KENTUCKY STORIES

by

Byron Crawford

Paducah, Kentucky

Copyright © 1994 by Byron Crawford

FIRST EDITION

Library of Congress Catalog Card Number: 94-61056
ISBN: 1-56311-166-7

Published by
Turner Publishing Company
412 Broadway
P.O. Box 3101
Paducah, KY 42001

Credits

Byron Crawford, Author

Design & Production: *Jim Erskine*
Photo Editor: *Cindy Stucky*
Copy Editor: *Carla Harris Carlton*
Story Editor: *Jackie Crawford*

Archival Research: *Lisa Barker, Sharon Bidwell, Patrick Chapman, Eric Crawford, Amy Inskeep, Darryl Patton, Patsy Terrell, Judy Wadlington, Eddie Wooten*

Artwork: *Jim Erskine, Herman Wiederwhol*

Cover and Dust Jacket Design: *James Asher, Jim Erskine, Byron Crawford*

Publishing Consultant: *Douglas W. Sikes*

Project Coordinator: *Daren Ferguson*

Photo Credits

Page 6: Photo courtesy of Lawson family archives
Page 28: Paul Schuhmann
Page 36: Associated Press
Page 75: Billy Davis
Page 81: Larry Spitzer
Page 94: some school photographer
Page 96: Bill Luster
Page 98: Photo courtesy of Tommy Brown
Page 105: Photo courtesy of Mac Kilduff
Page 110: Courier-Journal archives
Page 119: Photo courtesy of Darryl Patton, Gadsden, AL
Page 121: Postcard courtesy of Anne Hood, Louisville
Page 142: Worth Ensminger
Page 148: Courier-Journal archives
Page 168: Photo courtesy of Bob Terrell
Page 172: Stewart Bowman
Page 176: J. D. Knoth, courtesy of James R. Adams & Associates
Page 202: Durell Hall
Page 214: Stewart Bowman (KY Highway 80)

All other photos by Byron Crawford.

Table of Contents

Foreword vii
Introduction ix

Essay on Life 1
Riley Goodin 3
A Bottle of Soda 5
Garrett Morgan, Inventor 7
The Goose House 10
George and Betsy Ross Pigg 12
Horse Trek 14
Chauncey Love 16
Dere Mr. Ralerode 19
Clocking Out 22
Water Moccasins 24
Tall Timber 26
Lost and Found 28
Poetry of Life 30
Custer's Kentuckians 33
Cawood 36
Fats 39
Tom Harbut 42
Old Friends 45
Time Travel 47
Going Down to Dumas Walker's 49
Secretariat 51
Family Trees 54
Barn Clock 56
Rock Fence Maker 59
On Fence Rows 61
Of Shakers and Brooms 63
Palace of Versailles (KY) 65
The Needle's Eye 67
The Oldest Postmaster 70
Vintage Valentines 72
Moonstruck 75
Last Rites: Fletcher White 77
Harm's Way 80
Paintings in Words 83

Milkweed Pods and Peach Pits 86
Fill 'Er Up 88
Floyd's Barber Shop 90
Buttercups 92
Fractured Reflections 94
Life After Football 96
Toe to Toe with Joe Louis 98
A Tarnished Memory 101
"Mac" Kilduff Remembers JFK 104
On Secret Pond 107
The 'Sleeping Prophet' 110
God's Ad Man 112
The ABC's of Nature 115
Kentucky Characters I 117
The Goat Man 119
Kentucky Characters II 122
Hog Wild 125
Out of Pocket 127
Up, Up and a Spray 129
Speedy Stalker 132
A Face in the Cloud 134
Bluegrass Savannas 136
Stump of Contention 138
The Siamese Car 140
Sitting Cow 142
A Turtle Twosome 144
Hot Wheels 146
Death Valley Scotty 148
Hard Rock Cafe 151
Bucking for Success 153
The Tyrone Bridge 155
Mussel-Shell Memorials 157
The Dueling Tree 159
Brushed by History 161
Bandboozled 164
Buffaloed 166
Locust Tree 168
Remembering Lum 'n' Abner 170
Milk Run 172
Russell Hudson 174
Building Memories 176

Looking for a Sign 178
Choctaw Academy 180
Accidental Petroleum 183
Blind Mystic 185
Bayou de Chien 188
Doctor Hook 190
Chalk Dust Memories 192
Falling into Fame 195
Ice Sisters 198
The Pear Tree 201
A Few Strands of Lights 203
How Santa Scored a Touchdown 205
A Legacy of Giving 207
The Chair that Came Back 209
A Little Girl's Gift 211

Foreword

by Barry Bingham, Jr.
Former Publisher
Courier-Journal

Byron Crawford's Courier-Journal column is easily addictive. Fortunately, it is also legal! He has collected some of his best works for this second book -- a perfect "fix" for Kentucky-lore junkies like me.

It turns out that Byron and I share one career experience. We both made the transition from broadcast to print journalism. Byron spent his early days reading copy for a Stanford radio station and later advanced to WCKY in Cincinnati and finally WHAS in Louisville. His television feature, *Sideroads,* was one of the station's most popular programming features. In March 1979, he joined the news staff of The Courier-Journal.

I made the move from WHAS to The Courier-Journal and Louisville Times in 1966. The first thing I discovered at the newspapers was that we were blessed with some trophy-writers. Among them were Allan Trout, Joe Creason, John Fetterman, Barry Bingham Sr. and John Ed Pearce. Trout was, by then, a senior deity reporting from Frankfort. They, and more recently Byron Crawford, all share a common blessing: an ear for the language and an eye that sees what the rest of us often overlook.

If daily newspaper journalism was a picture it would look like those connected dots in children's drawing books. It is an endless series of episodic events: disasters, politics, business, human interest, investigative reporting, sports and more disasters.

But some writers are able to see a different collection of dots and transform them into a panorama. With a series of stories and vignettes about the colorful, the unusual and the forgotten, they paint for us a tableau that is both rich and detailed. Historians of the future may well turn to these writings for a truer picture of the real world we lived in than to the jumble of facts, statistics and events in the daily news columns.

In this book you will find a number of Byron's contributions to this rare world of journalistic artistry. Other than his columns, I have something else to thank Byron for. Ever since I've been in the newspaper business I've collected quotations about the press. They come from such sages as Adlai Stevenson, Mark Twain, H.L. Mencken, Martin Luther and Byron Crawford. Byron's is the briefest, only three words. "Mistakes love newsprint." How right he is.

But newsprint loves those words and phrases that can make a reader laugh, muse or cry. Byron has contributed many of them, and they're trophies worthy of this collection.

Introduction

In 1974, while most other reporters at WHAS-TV in Louisville were chasing police cars, fire trucks and politicians, I got sidetracked.

Photographer Haywood "Woody" Nichols and I found ourselves more drawn to an artist painting wildflowers in a mountain meadow, or to an old-timer spinning a tale of buried gold. We soared with glider pilots, fished with old river men, waded streams with barefoot youngsters catching crawdads, and hiked into the log woods with a boy who made sounds like a chain saw.

Viewers enjoyed the stories as much as we did, and soon we were producing a syndicated human interest feature series, called "Sideroads," for the news broadcasts on WHAS-TV and for WKYT-TV in Lexington, KET and stations in Tennessee and Ohio.

Although I switched from television to the Courier-Journal in 1979, my favorite subjects are still the ones that drew Woody and me to the sideroads in our television days. Woody is now with NBC in Miami, and Phil Martin, the other fine photographer with whom I worked, is with WSB-TV in Atlanta. But I am still here in Kentucky, where many of the roads are now as familiar to me as the long white gravel lane, with the ridge of grass in the middle, that I followed home from the school bus stop in Lincoln County when I was a kid.

People often ask me, "How do you find all those stories you write?" Most are tips from readers who drop me notes, or call, or leave word at country stores where they know I stop. To all of you who have helped me over the years, these stories are for you.

There are a few whose wealth of story ideas and expertise in matters of Kentucky lore merit special mention: Ron Bland, Bagdad; C. David Coffman, Liberty; Dave Long, Hustonville; Dave Watson, Plummers Landing; Nancy Farmer, Cynthiana; R. B. Campbell, Hyden, and Charles Wilson, Elkton; Joanne Hobbs, Athertonville; Howard Howells II and the late Col. George Chinn, Harrodsburg; Mary Lee, Whitley City; Shirley Sheperson, Forkland; Clemens Caldwell and Ralph Cress, Danville; Ike Adams, Paint Lick; Jodie Hall, Leitchfield; Leo Mudd, Clarkson; Jane Burkhead, Campbellsburg; James Riley, Benton; Bill Reed, Lexington; Stan Lemaster, Louisville; Kenny Vaughn and Danny Foley, Russell Springs.

I thank the Courier-Journal for permission to compile this book from previously published columns; former publisher Barry Bingham Jr. and former CBS News correspondent Charles Kuralt, who have risked their professional credibility by writing forewords for my books; Jim Erskine, President of The Kentucky Writers Association, for his advice; and my wife, Jackie, and our children, Eric, Andrea, Joe and Wes for their patience and understanding. I thank, too, my parents, Delbert and Lucille Crawford, who gave me the freedom, as a boy, to roam the woodlands and streams of central Kentucky -- where my imagination came to life and my mind's camera snapped many pictures that I am still putting into words.

-- B.C.

Essay on Life

June 15, 1992

"If I Had My Life To Live Over..."

The words, in bold type on the back of a newsletter sent to me by a management club in Calvert City, Ky., caught my eye, and I read on:

"I'd like to make more mistakes next time. I'd relax. I would limber up. I would be sillier than I have been this trip. I would take fewer things seriously. I would take more chances. I would climb more mountains and swim more rivers. I would eat more ice cream and less beans. I would perhaps have more actual troubles, but...fewer imaginary ones.

"You see, I'm one of those people who lives sensibly and sanely, hour after hour, day after day. Oh, I've had my moments, and if I had it to do over again, I'd have more of them. In fact, I'd try to have nothing else. Just moments, one after another, instead of living so many years ahead of each day. I've been one of those persons who never goes anywhere without a thermometer, a hot-water bottle, a raincoat and a parachute. If I had to do it again, I would travel lighter than I have.

"If I had my life to live over, I would start barefoot earlier in the spring and stay that way later in the fall. I would go to more dances. I would ride more merry-go-rounds. I would pick more daisies.

"Nadine Stair,
85 years old,
Louisville, Kentucky"

No sooner had I read the words than I thumbed through the Louisville phone directory hoping to find Nadine Stair's name, so I could call her and tell her what a wonderful thing she had written. But her name was not there.

In fact, there were only two listings under Stair, one of them attorney Fred Stair, whose office I called. He was out, but a secretary told me to phone his mother, General Laura Stair, who might be able to help.

It was not the first call she had gotten about the essay attributed to Nadine Stair, said General Stair, a retired teacher who owns

1

parking lots and other property around Churchill Downs. In fact, Stair said, she has been getting at least one call a week, and often more, for about 14 years from people all over the United States trying to reach Nadine Stair to ask permission to reprint the article or to congratulate the writer.

Several years passed before General Stair learned that the author's true identity was Nadine Strain.

Then one day either Stair or her daughter overheard the name Nadine Strain mentioned in a conversation about pipe organs or pump organs, Stair said. On the off chance that she might have been the mystery writer, they found Nadine Strain's name in the phone book and called to ask.

It turned out that she was the author of the essay and that her name had been misspelled "Stair" when the piece originally appeared in "Family Circle" on March 27th, 1978.

Stair said she got the impression from speaking with Nadine Strain on the phone that Strain was a very humble person, quite surprised that her little essay on living had generated so many phone calls for so long to a wrong number. Nadine Strain never mentioned writing anything else for publication, Stair said.

She and Strain never met, except on the phone, but Stair said she knew that Strain was an accomplished pianist and organist, that she had lived in the Crescent Hill section of Louisville, and that she had been active in a senior citizens' theater group.

Nadine Strain died at a nursing home in November 1988 and left her body to the University of Louisville School of Medicine. But she left little pieces of her heart and soul with all of us who have read her precious essay about eating ice cream, going barefoot, riding merry-go-rounds, picking daisies...and living life.

We will not forget you, Nadine Strain.

Riley Goodin

August 22, 1988

PINEVILLE, Ky. -- Bell County's most popular lawman carries a .38-caliber pistol on his hip and a crutch under each arm.

Pineville 1st District Constable Riley Goodin, who says he is 80, is now serving his fifth consecutive four-year term with an apparent lifetime lock on the unpaid position.

Nearly all night, every night, seven days a week, Goodin patrols downtown Pineville on foot, shuffling along on his crutches, his handcuffs rattling on his belt and his old pipe spewing smoke from a smoldering bowl of Bull Durham.

"I stay up till 3 or 4 o'clock," he said. "I get everything tied down, then I go in. I get up about 9 or 10 in the morning."

He lives in a room in downtown Pineville, behind the stores that he guards every night.

No one knows much about his early years, except that he was born in Pineville. He has never been married, and the only family he has is a sister who also lives in town. Life has not been easy for Riley Goodin. That much is told in his tired face and bent frame. But there is a spark in his eyes that shines only from the souls of men who are happy deep inside.

His dedication and warm personality have won the unwavering loyalty of a constituency that has been electing him by substantial margins since 1969. Even in 1982 -- when he forgot his party affiliation and registered for election on the Republican instead of the Democratic ticket -- Goodin still won.

On the streets of Pineville, a town of about 2,600, he is accorded the status of the true folk hero that he is. He never tires of hearing the story retold of how he once arrested a drunk and wheeled him off to jail in an abandoned grocery cart. He sometimes laughs aloud when men-folk around town allow him to demonstrate his viselike grip by extending their hands and wincing when he squeezes.

He has been shot twice, but only once in the line of duty. He was wounded in the abdomen several years ago when he tangled with a would-be robber at a local business.

The other wound occurred years before, at a time when Goodin used to kill hogs for people around Bell County. He was preparing to butcher a hog for a woman when the hog attacked him. The woman grabbed a gun and shot the animal, but the bullet traveled through the hog and through Goodin's knee, as well.

"She didn't mean to hit me," Goodin said. "It was my fault."

Although Goodin draws a small public-assistance check, he often gets his meals free from local businesses that appreciate his vigilance.

"Most men in the position he's in would be invalids, confined to some bed," said Pineville attorney Grant Knuckles. "I just like him."

Knuckles isn't alone in his admiration for the man whose name and reputation are so wonderfully matched.

"Everybody just loves him," said Britt Nelson, a Daily News reporter in Middlesboro. "He's got a real good heart and a good spirit about him that just overwhelms me."

For a good many years, Goodin used to gather up all the stray grocery carts from the A&P store in Pineville, tie them together and take them back to the store from all over town. "He's not hardly able to do that anymore," said Shirley Turner, the bookkeeper at the A&P. "Now, he pushes a little cart that he built himself, and he picks up cans off the road."

Grover Brock of Arnett Funeral Home in Pineville says he sees Goodin on patrol, often at 2 or 3 o'clock in the morning, winter and summer, during rain and snow.

Pineville illustrator Mason Combs, who has sketched or painted dozens of pictures of Goodin, has been quoted as saying that the aged lawman is John Wayne, Clint Eastwood, Marshal Dillon and Wyatt Earp all rolled into one.

"Yep, they know me in Cincinnati, Ohio, and different places that way," Goodin said. "If you ever have trouble around here, I'll help you out."

A Bottle of Soda

August 28, 1992

WILLIAMSBURG, Ky. -- The bottle of strawberry soda that Tom Henry Lawson walked eight miles or more to bring to his young wife, Nadine, on March 19, 1918, has never been opened.

Nadine and Tom Henry had been married three years then. She was 19 and he was 24. Their first baby was due any day.

They lived way back on Maple Creek in eastern Whitley County, at least four miles across a steep mountain from the nearest store. Nadine had a craving for strawberry soda that day, and Tom Henry's heart overruled his better judgment when he gave in to her pleas for a bottle from the store.

He set out across the mountain on foot, following a path that would get him to the store and back much quicker than he could have made the trip on horseback.

But when he returned with the strawberry soda, he found that Nadine had gone into labor while he was away, that there had been complications, and that both she and the baby girl had died during childbirth.

They were laid to rest in the Whetstone Cemetery, beside a little white church on a hill in Whitley County, and soon afterward, Tom Henry Lawson carried his grief away to World War I in France.

Upon his return to Whitley County, he remarried and started another family, but he always kept the unopened bottle of strawberry soda he had bought for Nadine sitting on top of the old parlor organ that had been hers, and that he and his second wife, Martha Ann, kept in their home. The organ was finally destroyed in a fire, but the bottle of strawberry soda was saved.

Pruda Lawson Mosley, 60, of Williamsburg, the youngest of eight children born to Tom Henry and Martha Ann Lawson, recalled that she and her brothers and sisters were not allowed to touch the bottle and that it was always treated with reverence in their home.

Mosley does not recall her father, a farmer and fur buyer, ever talking much about Nadine or the bottle of strawberry soda, but she is certain that Nadine's death was a source of much sorrow throughout his life.

"From what my oldest sister said, Daddy must have loved her a lot," Mosley reflected. "I picture her as being a gentle, pretty, soft-spoken woman. My daddy was a good-looking man, and for those times back then I'd say she was one of the prettiest of women. I'm sure her hair was dark brown, and I think she had brown eyes and a dark complexion."

Tom Henry Lawson died in 1965 at age 71 of a heart ailment that had developed soon after Nadine's death. He was buried beside Nadine and their baby. Martha Ann, who died in 1972, was buried on the other side of him.

Pruda Mosley now has the unopened strawberry soda, bottled by the old Nelson Carbonating Works of Jellico, Tenn., the contents of which have evaporated by about one-third over the past 74 years.

She has kept the bottle mostly because it seemed so special to her father, Mosley said. Perhaps Tom Henry Lawson held onto the bottle as a reminder to never again let his heart overrule his good judgment.

Or maybe he saw in the dusty old bottle a last smile from that pretty face, or felt a last kiss, or heard Nadine's last "I love you" as he walked away up the mountain path in 1918, with just enough change in his pocket to buy the last thing she ever told him she wanted.

Garrett Morgan, Inventor

January 22, 1986

PARIS, Ky. -- In the summer of 1895, at the age of 18, Garrett Morgan, a native of Paris in Bourbon County, arrived in Cleveland with one dime in his pocket and only an elementary school education.

The seventh of 11 children, Morgan had been on his own since age 14, when he left Paris and moved to Cincinnati to work as a handyman.

But young Morgan had dreams of greater things, and it was not long before they began to materialize.

He taught himself enough about the sewing machine that he was able to find a job as a machine adjuster, first with Roots & McBride in Cleveland, and later, with other companies.

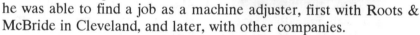

Within 12 years, he had gone into business for himself in a shop that sold and repaired sewing machines, had bought a home and moved his mother to Cleveland.

Two years later, he opened a tailoring shop that employed 32 people. There he encountered a problem that led to his first invention.

The sewing machine needles moved up and down so rapidly that friction heat often scorched the thread of woolen materials. Morgan set about to find a chemical solution that could be applied to the needles to reduce friction.

One night his wife called Morgan to dinner while he was in the middle of an experiment, and he wiped the chemicals from his hands on a piece of wiry, pony-fur cloth.

When he returned from dinner, he noticed that the fuzz of the cloth on which he had wiped his hands was straight. He tried the chemical treatment on his neighbor's Airedale dog, and again the curly hair was straightened.

Morgan then tried the solution on his own hair, a little at a time at first, then on his whole head, the result being the first human-hair straightener, which was marketed as G.A. Morgan Hair Refining Cream.

It was to be the first of many successful inventions for the Kentuckian.

In 1912, Morgan introduced the safety hood -- forerunner of the gas-mask -- for which he received a patent in 1914. His invention won wide acclaim in 1916 when an explosion in crib No. 5 of the Cleveland water works, 250 feet below Lake Erie, trapped 32 workmen in a tunnel filled with dust, smoke and poisonous gases.

Morgan and his brother, Frank, were summoned to the scene, where they donned the safety hoods and entered the tunnel. Although some of the trapped men died, all were brought out of the tunnel, and newspapers all over the nation carried the story of the Morgans' heroism.

Garrett Morgan was later awarded a gold, diamond-studded medal proclaiming him Cleveland's "most honored and bravest citizen," along with a medal and honorary membership in the International Association of Fire Engineers.

During World War I, a modified version of Morgan's invention emerged as the gas mask.

Within a few years, Morgan, after witnessing a traffic accident between an automobile and a horse-drawn carriage at a Cleveland intersection, came up with another well-known safety device -- the tri-colored traffic signal light.

He patented the traffic signal in November 1923, and secured British and Canadian patents as well.

The rights to his traffic signal were bought by the General Electric Company for $40,000, a large sum at that time.

Among his other inventions were a woman's hat fastener, a round belt fastener and a friction drive clutch.

He is also credited with founding the Cleveland Call newspaper, later known as the Call & Post, which was devoted primarily to coverage of black affairs in Cleveland, whose circulation territory eventually extended to Columbus and Cincinnati.

Louis Haber's book, *Black Pioneers of Science and Invention*, characterized Morgan as a jolly man, quick-tempered and outspoken, whose friends included John D. Rockefeller Sr.

Although Morgan spent his life in Cleveland, where he and his wife raised three sons, he did return to his hometown of Paris occasionally, recalled 85-year-old Lawrence Kellis of Paris.

"I remember Morgan coming down here when I was in high school, I'd say about 1914, and demonstrating his gas mask," Kellis said. "He'd come down here around Decoration Day."

Several years ago, the Claysville section of Paris was renamed Garrett Morgan Place and a historical marker was erected in his memory.

Morgan died at Cleveland in 1963 at the age of 86.

The Goose House

April 28, 1986

HAZARD, Ky. -- One of Perry County's best-known landmarks is a house with a roof that resembles a goose and eight windows that are egg-shaped.

It is on the east end of town, on a knoll overlooking Main Street. An engraved keystone over the front door bears the name "Mother Goose" and the date 1940, when the house was built.

The house was designed by George Stacy, a fireman on the old Louisville & Nashville Railroad Co. Stacy lived there until his death 32 years ago. His wife, Ollie, 83, lived there until moving to Ohio eight years ago. She still owns the house and adjacent buildings, which house a grocery known as the Mother Goose Market and the Mother Goose restaurant.

"As far as I know, the goose was all my husband's idea," Mrs. Stacy said recently. "I have no idea how he came up with that notion. He should have been an architect; he was always coming up with something. I thought it was stupid half the time, but maybe it wasn't so bad after all."

She recalls that her husband and one of his friends, Ezekiel Smith, who owned the Maytag dealership in Hazard at the time, discussed trying to build a house for Smith in the shape of a Maytag wringer-type washing machine. However, the idea never materialized.

The exterior of the Mother Goose house is made of sandstone from creeks all over the area, most of it hauled to the site by Mrs. Stacy and the Stacys' three sons.

"It took us forever to build it. We'd work a while and build a while," Mrs. Stacy said.

Originally, the house was roofed with round, green shingles, but Mrs. Stacy couldn't find that kind of shingle the last time the house was roofed, so black, rectangular ones were used.

The head of the goose -- with eyes made of old automobile headlights that once blinked off and on -- is about 15 feet high. There is a tail at the other end of the roof.

The goose, which now serves as an office for the grocery, has three bedrooms, a living room, a kitchen and a bath.

It continues to be a conversation piece, and Sid Adams, who leases the house and the other buildings, says tourists still stop frequently to ask about the house and to take pictures.

"A group of Texans in a bus -- I mean like 40 -- stopped one time," Adams said. " This thing was in Car & Driver Magazine. They really had a good article about it. Everybody asks, 'What is it?' "

Adams and his sister, Tudy Cody, patiently tell visitors what they know about the house. Apparently, however, no one has ever figured out why George Stacy chose to make the roof of his home look like a goose, a fowl he never seemed particularly fond of, Mrs. Stacy said.

George and Betsy Ross Pigg

July 3, 1991

SHELBYVILLE, Ky. -- A television commercial keeps reminding me that the heartbeat of America is Chevrolet. Maybe so, but I think it is George and Betsy Ross Pigg.

George, a 57-year-old bachelor, runs a one-man barber shop on a side street in Shelbyville, and for more than 30 years he cared for his mother who recently entered a nursing home.

His sister, Betsy Ross Pigg, 65, was born on July 4th, works for the welfare department in Orange County, Calif., and makes flags for a hobby. She

was in the Navy shore patrol in World War II; never wears anything but red, white and blue; is a member of the American Legion and Daughters of the American Revolution; owns a small genealogical research company called "Are You A Pigg?"; and publishes a newsletter called "Pigg Tales."

I visit Pigg's Barber Shop now and then to swap funny stories with George and to remind myself that America still has a heartbeat.

George's VFW cap hangs in the shop's closet, and it can be put on at a moment's notice. Seldom is there a parade in Shelby County that George, the quartermaster of his VFW post, isn't there, wearing the cap and waiting for Old Glory to pass.

"I don't march in any parades because I've got a bad leg, but I coordinate the VFW marchers," George said. "I guess I'm kind of over-patriotic. Every time I hear the national anthem or 'America' -- any of those songs -- cold chills run up and down my spine. I always salute every flag that comes by, and the last parade we had here, I was the only one on the street that saluted."

12

An American flag sits in one corner of his barber shop -- midway between a big picture of two English setters on point and a large color poster of military awards and decorations. A sign in the window of the smoke-filled shop reads, "If you love freedom, thank a veteran."

"It hurt me. Two boys that got killed in Vietnam were my customers," George said. "I gave them a free haircut before they left."

George served in the Army during the occupation of Germany in the early 1950s, and he and many of his customers who are older veterans often relive their days in the military.

"I've got a deal that I offer -- if a man comes here and pays me to cut his hair the first hundred years, the second hundred, I give him free haircuts," Pigg said. "One man named Bert Scruggs lived to be 104 and got free haircuts four years."

George Pigg's one celebrity customer is sausage king Allen Purnell, a longtime friend, who lives in nearby Simpsonville.

Several weeks ago, when Betsy Ross Pigg was visiting her brother, I stopped by the barber shop and took their picture.

She is still making flags, she said, small ones with the stars and stripes made of different fabric so they can be enjoyed by the blind people to whom they are given.

The name Betsy Ross was her father's idea, Betsy said, and she likes it. She likes the name Pigg, too. So well, in fact, that after her divorce from a man named Farrell, she took back her original name.

I took a good look at them standing there with the flag, waiting for me to snap their picture -- Betsy dressed in red, white and blue from head to toe, making flags for blind people to feel, and George in his VFW cap, waiting anxiously for the next parade, so he can salute Old Glory.

America's heart is still beating.

Horse Trek

July 30, 1990

VERSAILLES, Ky. -- Actor William Shatner and his wife, Marcy, of Los Angeles say they now consider themselves Kentuckians.

Shatner, best known as Capt. James Kirk of television and motion-picture "Star Trek" fame, owns a 76-acre horse farm in Woodford County where he raises and trains American Saddlebreds.

"I am a Kentuckian," Shatner insists. "I own property here. I'm here all the time. I've acquired a Kentucky accent and I'm a Kentucky Colonel. So I don't know what other qual-

ifications you'd need, other than being born here."

Shatner was breeding quarter horses in California six years ago when he became familiar with the American Saddlebred and "fell in love with the breed."

A California trainer introduced him to Donna Moore, a well-known Kentucky saddlebred rider and trainer, who assisted Shatner in buying several horses and who now manages his farm -- Belle Reve.

"I bought a stallion, under her direction, named Sultan's Great Day, which has turned out to be, through a series of excellent choices on her part and an element of good luck, one of the great breeding stallions," Shatner said.

Increasingly, Shatner the actor is gaining a reputation among veterans in the saddlebred business as Shatner the horseman, not only for his passion for saddlebreds, but also for his riding ability and knowledge of the animals.

Many American Saddlebred shows now include a western pleasure horse class known as the Shatner Class, named after the actor.

"I've paid my dues over several years of humiliation and financial losses, and have stuck it out," Shatner said with a grin. "It has not been given to me. And in the ring, I sense that judges may require more of me, because they don't want it to appear that I'm being given something because I may have a higher profile."

Renowned trainer Redd Crabtree of Simpsonville said he has never seen anyone enter the saddlebred business and give as selflessly as Shatner, whom he called a credit to the industry.

Shatner is also known as an all-around nice guy in Woodford County. Last year, he showed up in Versailles to present trophies to participants in a small fund-raising marathon for a drug-free society.

"I'm a landowner in Woodford County, and the chief of police in Versailles -- whose nickname is Squirrel -- asked me to do it," Shatner said. "How can you refuse a guy with the nickname of Squirrel?"

Shatner and his wife will ride at this year's World Championship Horse Show at the Kentucky State Fair in August. The two usually also ride in several smaller shows around the state each year.

A horse ridden by Marcy Shatner finished first in the amateur three-gaited stake Saturday night at the Mercer County Fair and Horse Show in Harrodsburg; William Shatner's horse finished second in the five-gaited grand championship, which was won by Mercer Countian Tom Moore.

"I'm going to be in New York this week, and they wanted me to do the David Letterman show on Friday night, but I decided I'd rather do the Danville (Boyle County) Fair Horse Show," said Shatner, who will fly back to Kentucky to ride in the event.

The actor says that, to his gratification, he is being asked more and more about the breeding of saddle horses these days, in addition to the questions he always gets about "Star Trek."

"Leonard Nimoy (Mr. Spock) and I are very good friends, and so is DeForest Kelley, who played Dr. McCoy," Shatner said. However, his trusted space sidekicks do not share his passion for horses.

"Everybody's business manager says, 'Do not buy anything that eats while you sleep.' "

Chauncey Love

April 18, 1988

DANVILLE, Ky. -- His Southern Kentucky drawl is as smooth as a locomotive whistle, and when he tells a railroad story you sometimes can almost see moonlight dancing on the tracks.

H.C. "Chauncey" Love, 70, a retired Southern Railway conductor, is what you might call a natural-born railroader. His grandfather, Dunn, was a brakeman, and his father, John Henry, was a carman on the Southern.

Love was born on the edge of Somerset, but while he was still a boy, he and his family lived for several years in Ludlow, across the Ohio River from Cincinnati, where Southern had a roundhouse.

Love said people used to joke that so many Southern Kentucky railroaders were in Ludlow because of a tunnel: "They used to say that when they bored the hole for the Kings Mountain tunnel (in Lincoln County), it turned everybody loose, and they took Ludlow without a shot."

In the years between 1939, when Love went to work for the railroad, and 1983, when he retired, the tracks between Cincinnati and Chattanooga were his home away from home. When Love was on the train, things were never dull.

He regularly bought newspapers to toss out the caboose windows to people who waited faithfully along the tracks and waved to him. Then there were the ventriloquist's dummies that Love and his father carried to entertain railroaders and people who lived along the tracks.

"The old man's dummy was named Jerry O'Riley Appletree," Love recalled. "We took some soot off a skillet and blacked his eye, and the old man was always telling that Ora -- that was my mother -- blacked his eye.

"People would say, 'How'd that happen?' And the dummy would say, 'She throwed a skillet at John Henry, and he dodged.' "

Love continued with a laugh: "When he first got him, he'd get in front of a mirror and practice. Sometimes the dummy would be moving his lips and not saying anything. It wasn't synchronized."

The younger Love's dummy was named Jack Nack. "He was brown-headed and block-headed, and he had an eyelid that you could work ...and he'd wink. I'd catch these girls ...and I'd get Jack Nack to wink at 'em," Love said.

"A feller bought him a rubber bow tie with two light bulbs on it, and had a battery down in it. And when they'd get ahold of his hand, I'd make that bow tie light up."

"I'd stick that dummy's head out the caboose window, and then I'd holler," Love said. "These section men would put their hands up and shade their eyes and look and look till the caboose went out of sight.

"One feller that knew me said one man had said, after we went by, 'They must be hiring some new men.' And another one said, 'Yeah, and they're ugly as hell.' "

Love also went through a spell of banjo playing during his early years on the railroad. He played three days and nights one time for a New Year's party at a beer joint in Northern Kentucky.

But he finally went away to World War II, then got married, and eventually both Jack Nack and his banjo got away from him.

For 10 years before his retirement, Love was the oldest conductor on the Southern Railway. His uniform still hangs in a closet at his Danville home, and his mind is a library of railroad history and humor.

"Let me tell you this one: That youngest brother of mine, Lloyd Ernie, who's dead now, decided to go to Texas when he was about 16.

"My Daddy said, 'All right, but I know you won't write me when you get down there, and I'm aimin' to write a letter, and when you get off that train down there, I want you to mail it. That way, I'll know you've got down there.' "

Their father spent a good while writing the letter, addressing the envelope and sealing it.

As they waited for the train, he handed the letter to Lloyd Ernie with a reminder to mail it when he reached Houston. "What does the letter say?" Lloyd Ernie asked.

"----, how would I know, Lloyd Ernie!" his father exclaimed. "I ain't got it yet."

When the letter arrived a few days later, his father happily tore it open and began reading: "Dear folks, I am fine. How is everyone back home? I miss you all. How is the weather? ..."

Dere Mr. Ralerode

November 7, 1988

Today's column is dedicated to the many of you who have written to me since December 1981 -- and are still writing -- requesting an encore of my "Dere Mr. Ralerode," column, which was a reprint of an item from a 1937 edition of the "Kentucky State Bar Journal."

Attorney Edwin L. Cohen of Louisville gave me the item in hopes that readers would enjoy it, and apparently you have.

It seems that when the Paducah, Tennessee and Alabama Railroad was built through Marshall, Calloway and other Western Kentucky and West Tennessee counties, it traversed an almost unbroken forest and vast grazing lands teeming with cattle, hogs and other livestock, a great number of which were killed by trains, causing the railroad no end of trouble.

There was, at that time, a young attorney in Murray named Burrell B. Linn, a smooth-spoken, diplomatic and friendly chap, with a flair for getting along with farmers. Linn was retained as a claim agent for the railroad.

It is recorded that, back in the 1890s, when a train ran over and killed six people, he settled the entire claim out of court for $150 per person.

But at last he met his match, when a train struck a Tennessee farmer's pet bull. The following is said to be an exact copy of a letter the farmer wrote to the vice president of the railroad:

> *Mr. A. H. Dauchy, V. Prst. of yure ralerode;*
> *Dere Sir:*
> *This is the third letter I have writ you in regardst to my clame for enjury of my spotted bull, a pet of my fambly, which we named Daniel Webster, but which we called Buster for short.*
> *I already told you twisct that yure trane hit my bull a-tween Holler Rock Junction and the second mile post comen this way. No reply from you except you sent me a blank to fill out -- and dam the blank. A Filerdelphia lawyer could not fill hit out.*
> *As I said before frum whare the trane hit the bull it carried him a right smart peace beyond that pint. I tole you plane that the injine tore offen a peace of his hide averagen eight inches from his under lip then sorto zagonal over his shoulder and back, and then down his left side clear under to his nable on below part of his body.*

19

The trane wheel also stripped off part of his hind hufes smack and smooth maken his fet very tender and sore so he can not walk good without me and my boy Joe holden him up with a pole when he travils to pond for water which is only about two rods off from where he is.

Before this axident he was a very threatening beast and mighty cantankerous. Since then he has a sad look and bawls most of the time, princepally at night disturbing us considerable. He don't eat scarcely anything except some dry meal because his jaws is mighty sore.

Tow of my nebors who I do not speak to say they will swar that this bull was struck by lighteen but they are a dam lie. He was hit by yure payoff speshial trane which come through my field a gallahooten at midnight of Mch. of the 20 with its whissle a screamen like hell.

Now if nothin was hitten by this trane why was it screamen like hell? You can't answer. Neither can they. Nor nobody.

Now lissen right clost. Me and Henry Hefferman has aprazed this bull of value at $eighteen dollars and six bits and he is as we say beyond doubtless a totle loss. Henry says he aint never saw sich damage to a bull in his day and time, and neither have I and my boy Joe says the same and we all say he will never be any more use for a bull hardly not even for befe.

So take notice of this. This is writ on Friday and maled on North bound trane. Onlessen I receve check in full . . . by a Thursday next I heard some people say that sum spikes are agoing to git loost from the rales of yure rode which will cause the rales to spred out when yure passenger trane number 104 cums along.

Then thar will be some big hedlines in the paducky papers saying that sum coches went into the barpit in my feld, that a injineer and farman were kilt and hurten sum passengers right bad and maybe yure dam conductor Aleck Fulton will get a leg broke or both legs and I don't give a dam for that either.

Further and more to that you nede not send that Pot bellied burl Linn yure clame agt. down here to settle with me and maybe talk me out of the whole buseness with honey words and honey words don't git no bakon at Stagners store over at Holler Rock Junction.

So you better send on the check as I advice you for I aint in no state of mind to be talked to or have my word disputen nor written you leters which don't git no answer.

P. S. Jest a slite hint. Effen you think you will git this case in Judge Harewoods cote you are offen your nut. Him and yure clame agt. is as thick as theves and I wuld sware him offen the bench in a minute for I seen him and yure clame agt. a playing pich trumps in Shorty Dugans sody warter place for sody warter they said but I guess it were for sumpin stronger for Shortys place aint nothen more or less than a salune and Shorty hisself saw this game if he will stick to what he said, which I very much doubt as burds of a fether always floch together in the cote house and I don't mean maybe.

Git that and git it good for you cant mess with me no longer.

The farmer got his check on the next train by special delivery, and claim agent Linn was later quoted as saying that if there had been air mail in those days, the check would have arrived within the hour.

Clocking Out
April 4, 1988

STANFORD, Ky. -- Yesterday, when everyone else in Kentucky set their clocks ahead one hour in observance of daylight-saving time, Robert Matheny's timepieces stayed right where they have been for 40-odd years, meaning that they are now two hours behind everyone else's in Lincoln County.

One of his lost hours will be recovered when clocks are turned back in October, but the other hour was lost when Matheny refused to switch from Central to Eastern time -- first during World War II, then

permanently when the Eastern time zone was enlarged to include parts of Eastern and Central Kentucky and Tennessee.

"I don't remember exactly when we went on fast time, but it was back when old Roosevelt went in, and it's ruined the whole damn country," Matheny complained. "I never have changed my time since it started. I'm on the time that I was born on, back before the boundary lines changed."

Matheny, 76, and his wife, Beatrice, own and operate a 268-acre farm a few miles south of Stanford, where Matheny sometimes is in the field from sunup to sundown, working on what he calls "slow time."

"You can't get the cows up on fast time; chickens don't go to roost. And what burns me up, I go down here and get these boys to work and it'll be good, dry, hay-baling time, you know, everything's running sweet.

"Here comes along 3 o'clock, by my time, and they'll say, 'We've got to quit, it's 5 o'clock.' Well, from 3 on till 6 or 7 o'clock, you've got three or four good hours running there, and me paying them by the hour. But they've got their watch moved up, and it's 5 o'clock. But by my time it's 3 o'clock.

"A lot of 'em I just tell 'em, 'When you go, you're gone.' "

Although Matheny laughs at himself occasionally, he makes no apologies for his fierce independence, which has been tested several times over the years.

He used to milk 25 cows by hand twice a day until the milk company tried to force him to invest in some new equipment by threatening to stop buying his milk.

"I said, 'Brother, that's the best ...thing I've heard. Make this the last milk you pick up,' " Matheny recalled. And he got out of the dairy business.

"They said, 'Oh, you can't do that.'

"I said, 'Well it looks to me like I can do it. These are my cows, and this is my place.'

"You're young and you may live to see it," he told me. "One of these days, this country will wake up hungry. Watch what I'm telling you."

He pulled from his bib-overalls pocket a Waltham pocket watch that he's been carrying for 50 years.

"It's only got one gear in it," he said. "What would I gain by changing it? The sun comes up and goes down just the same on your time as it does on mine.

"Course, my time's about out anyway. I'll be 77, if I live to see it, the 11th of May at 10:30 ...my time."

Water Moccasins
July 15, 1988

LAFFOON, Ky. -- A swamp on the backwaters of Panther Creek in eastern Daviess County holds the dubious distinction of being the easternmost habitat in Kentucky for cottonmouth water moccasins.

Although harmless water snakes are often mistaken for the poisonous cottonmouth, herpetologist Bob Todd of Sonora, who has been charting the location of cottonmouths and other reptiles in Kentucky since 1961, says cottonmouths have never been officially verified east of the Daviess County site.

"Initially, it was thought they were in every county in the state," Todd said. "Then it was thought that they were only at Murphy's Pond (a cypress swamp in Hickman County). Then, after that, we found a few in other counties. But there are a lot of counties, even in the western part of the state, where you don't find them."

Besides Daviess and Hickman counties, Todd says cottonmouths have also been found in the backwaters of Mud River in southwestern Butler County, in Union County, at two sites in Muhlenberg County, in Fulton County on the northern end of Reelfoot Lake and occasionally around Kentucky Lake in Calloway and Marshall.

Todd is puzzled about why he is unable to find cottonmouths in Henderson or Ohio counties despite perfect habitat and the counties' proximity to other sites where cottonmouths have been confirmed.

Western Kentucky and southern Illinois -- along the Mississippi River -- are at the northern tip of the cottonmouth's natural range. It is predominant in the swamps and bayous of the deep South. On May 5, 1983, according to Todd, the first cottonmouth on record in

Indiana was found in a swamp on the outskirts of Jasper in Dubois County about 35 miles northeast of Owensboro, Ky.

Contrary to a popular myth that the cottonmouth is aggressive, Todd, who has captured several hundred of them over the years, says the snake is docile. Still, the cottonmouth is less apt to crawl or swim away than an ordinary water snake when approached by a human.

While harmless water snakes may sometimes resemble the cottonmouth -- brown with broad, dark olive bands -- there are several distinguishing characteristics.

The water snake's pupil is round, while the cottonmouth's is elliptical, like a cat's. Cottonmouths also have a pit, or hollow, on the side of the head in front of the eye, just below eye level. "Another thing," Todd said, "if you look down on a water snake's head from straight above him, you can see his eyes very prominently. A cottonmouth's you can't because there's a big scale that sets out over them."

The cottonmouth is so called because the inside of its mouth is supposed to be whiter than that of other snakes, but Todd says the difference isn't that noticeable.

Although the cottonmouth is a cousin of the copperhead, its venom is more comparable to that of the rattlesnake.

"Copperhead venom is the least poisonous of all of them," Todd said. "You'll make a lot of people mad if you say that, but I've seen a study where they kept a 10-year record on copperhead bites. I think there were about 309 bites, and over half of them had no treatment whatsoever, and no deaths at all."

Todd says the severity of any poisonous snakebite often depends on the size of the snake. Larger snakes usually produce more venom and, thus, inflict more serious bites.

Todd has been bitten twice by small cottonmouths, but with only minor discomfort.

Several years ago, Todd caught the largest cottonmouth ever recorded in Kentucky -- 47 1/4 inches long, weighing 5 1/4 pounds -- in Butler County.

Several times, he says, he has counted as many as 30 cottonmouths during one trip through the 40-acre swamp in Daviess County.

Tall Timber

February 27, 1991

PARKERS LAKE, Ky. -- Kentucky's tallest tree and its largest yellow poplar are one magnificent specimen that towers over a secluded nest of virgin timber in the rugged and beautiful wilderness of southeastern Kentucky.

The tree, discovered in 1971 by Clemon Garrison of the U.S. Forest Service Somerset Ranger Station, is 174 feet tall and measures 70 inches in diameter at the standard point of measurement -- 41/2 feet from its base.

Garrison believes the tree owes its survival mostly to its location -- several miles from civilization in the Daniel Boone National Forest in northern McCreary County. The tree is nearly surrounded by sheer gray sandstone cliffs, in a shady gorge littered with large, moss-covered boulders, where removing it would be nearly impossible.

Here the big poplar has passed the centuries in relative obscurity since well before the long hunters first smiled upon the territory that was to be Kentucky.

The distant splattering of waterfalls and the lonesome calls of logcocks and wild turkeys still ricochet through the sanctuary of giant hardwoods, where the poplar and its companions have escaped lightning, wind, fire and human predators since they were saplings.

So inaccessible is the site that a cliff must be scaled to reach the massive poplar.

"In my opinion, there is more true wilderness here -- the way it was before Daniel Boone came -- than anywhere else in Kentucky," Garrison said, making his way toward the tree.

"You don't get the magnitude of this tree until you get to within about 12 feet of it. The volume in the first 16-foot log would be 4,356 board feet."

Many early Kentucky homes and other structures were built with yellow poplar lumber because of its natural abundance, easy workability and its reputed termite resistance.

Most of Kentucky's virgin poplar forests had been harvested commercially by the turn of the century, but a few trees survived the logging to remind us of what Kentucky once was.

Garrison is reluctant to estimate the age of the giant yellow poplar in McCreary County, but he guesses it to be about 300 years. It is still growing, although very slowly, he says. Between 1975 and 1980, its girth expanded one inch. Given its apparent good health and safe hiding place, foresters believe the big poplar might survive for many more years.

With some luck, maybe it will stand through another few centuries, to be rediscovered by each new generation; a living monument to what nature can do when left alone.

Lost and Found

January 15, 1990

"Unbelievable" is how Dr. Carroll Witten of Louisville describes the news that his prisoner-of-war tag, lost in Germany in January 1945, had been found and was being returned to him.

It was among the dozens of small miracles that occurred when the Berlin Wall was opened Nov. 9.

On the Sunday after the historic opening, an East German family who had never been in West Germany approached U. S. Army Capt. James Allen on a street in West Berlin and gave him a tarnished brass tag, bearing only a four-digit prisoner-of-war number and the words "Oflag Luft 3," which Witten says was a designation for a prison camp for air officers.

The family told Allen, who is from Dallas, that they had found the tag in the rubble of their old barn, which had burned in 1988. "Probably they just thought somebody had died in the barn, but they couldn't find any bones," Witten explained.

In the next several days after he was given the tag, Allen, through the archives of the Red Cross office in Geneva, traced the number to Witten, 65, a family practitioner who served as president of the Louisville Board of Aldermen from 1969 through 1973.

Witten said that Allen phoned him in early December from Berlin, introduced himself and asked, "Were you in Germany?

"I said, 'Yes, I was a flier and was shot down there and captured.'

"He said, 'Do you know your prisoner number?'

"I said, 'Sure, I couldn't forget it . . . 4854.'

"He said, 'You're the guy.' "

The captain then explained to Witten how East Germany's Wilhelm Kostbush, his wife, two sons and daughter had brought the tag to West Berlin on their first visit.

Witten, who was a navigator on a B-17 bomber, was captured about five days after he bailed out when the plane was shot down over Saarbruecken, Germany, in May 1944.

In January 1945, Witten and some 40 other prisoners were being marched through deep snow and sub-zero temperatures from Zagan, Poland, to Bad Muskau, on the German border. Late in the evening they stopped at the barn to spend the night.

The next morning, Witten said, he noticed that his tag, worn on a chain around his neck, was missing. Fearing he might be punished for losing it, he did not tell the Germans, who never discovered the tag was gone.

Witten wondered about the missing tag several times over the years, he said, but he never dreamed it would be returned to him 45 years after the war, thousands of miles from the spot where he lost it.

Just before Christmas, Allen routed himself through Louisville on a flight from Germany to Dallas and gave the long-lost tag to its rightful owner.

"Allen didn't know the address of the people who found the tag," Witten said. "But their farm is 13 kilometers from Bad Muskau, and he's going to get their address from Germany and call me. I want to write them, and I'd like to go back to Germany, maybe in a year, and see them.

"It was a funny feeling when I held this tag in my hand again," Witten reflected. "Unbelievable."

Poetry of Life

October 18, 1991

MONTICELLO, Ky. -- In June of 1940, Edith Brewster wrote a little verse that she called "Things of Beauty."

"Two red heads against a background of green bushes. Little chickens following their mother in a clean-swept yard. The old dead peach tree, covered with trumpet vine blossoms. The snowball bush in full bloom in the front yard."

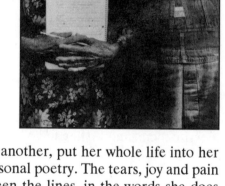

They were the simple, strong words of a woman struggling with the hardships of daily life, finding poetry in what beauty there was around her in a cabin on a hillside in Wayne County's Missouri Hollow, where she still lives.

She carried the stub of a pencil and a scrap of paper with her to work in the garden, to write down the thoughts that came to her. The pencil was still with her this summer in the garden where she grew enough vegetables to can 400 quarts.

The mother of 11 children, two of them deceased, Edith Brewster, 82, has, in one way or another, put her whole life into her plain, heartfelt and intensely personal poetry. The tears, joy and pain are all there -- sometimes between the lines, in the words she does not say. But there all the same.

In "Christmas 1986" she wrote:

Tonight my heart is lonely,
And tears come often to my eyes,
While I sit here sadly thinking,
As I do when my heart cries.

30

Many years at time of Christmas,
The birthday of our precious Lord,
Our home was filled with happy people,
And the promise of His word.

The promise in His word still fills me,
And He leads me just the same,
And the reason for my sadness,
All my children never came . . .

Why do I let this hurt me so,
When they're content to stay away?
Because I love them just the same,
As I did on their first birthday. . . .

Edith remembers that she was 8 years old when she wrote her first little rhyme, something about the weather.

When she was 13, her mother had a stroke that left her unable to move or speak, and Edith, the oldest of four children, was faced with caring for the family.

At age 17 she met and married Ed, her husband of 65 years, who now is 92 and nearly blind.

He worked in the log woods and at a sawmill most of his life. Looking back to the early 1930s, he doesn't know how they got by when he was making 35 cents an hour and he and Edith already had four children. Ed, one of 9 children whose mother died when he was 5, said he never learned to read or write. Edith finished the eighth grade.

Their daughter Minnie Evelyn died of typhoid at age 5 in 1932, but she is remembered at the age of 1 year in Edith's 'A Memory of 1928.'

One April day in early morn,
Before the sun was high,
A young mother hung her baby clothes,
Upon a line to dry.

High up in the apple tree,
A mocking bird looked on,
And after watching for a while,
He burst into a song.

As she listened to the music,
Coming from the songbird's throat,
She knows no sweeter notes could come,
That a music master wrote.

She brought her baby daughter,
To see the bird up in the tree.
Her little brown eyes sparkled,
And she clapped her hands with glee.

All through the spring and summer,
We watched and listened to the bird,
And I still call those morning concerts,
The best I've ever heard.

Tears welled up in Ed Brewster's eyes as he listened to the poem being read.

"Some of them will tickle you, and some will make you sad," he said.

A while back, Edith had about 100 of her poems printed in a small booklet that she titled "Poems and Ponderings," just to give to her family.

There are poems and messages in it for her children and grandchildren; her thoughts about rainy days and changing seasons, smiles and memories, love and laughter.

Ed Brewster held the little poem book close to his face, squinting to see Edith's picture on the page inside the front cover.

He thought she was a pretty woman, he said, "and a good one, too."

They stood for a picture in front of their little house in Missouri Hollow, Ed with his cap in his hand and Edith holding her pencil and a tattered notebook, with a lifetime of feelings inside.

Custer's Kentuckians

July 24, 1991

Gen. George Armstrong Custer's 7th Cavalry, whose legendary last stand at Montana's Little Big Horn River earned it a gilded page in history, counted several Kentuckians in its ranks.

Relatively little appears to have been written about them, but official records indicate that 16 to 19 Kentucky natives rode with Custer, that three of them were awarded the Medal of Honor, and that as many as 14 others in Custer's army enlisted in Kentucky, some of whom probably lived here.

Custer was stationed at Elizabethtown, Ky., from the fall of 1871 until 1873. There he commanded a small force that policed mostly Ku Klux Klan and illegal whiskey-making activities. In the spring of 1873 he left on the western expedition that ended in the fight with the Sioux and Cheyenne in 1876.

Most of the Kentucky troopers who rode with Custer were farm boys -- able horsemen and tough. Their ages ranged from about 21 to 45 and their height averaged about 5 feet, 8 inches -- typical of the "horse soldiers" of that day.

Despite the extensive historical research on Custer's last stand -- in which more than 220 of Custer's soldiers died -- much conflicting information exists about that day, June 25, 1876. This brief sketch of the Kentuckians who served, and their roles, is therefore subject to documented correction and clarification.

Most of the Kentucky soldiers not under Custer's personal command survived the Little Big Horn campaign, although several were wounded, and some killed, in other fighting during the pincer movement by Custer's commanders, Maj. M.A. Reno and Capt. F.W. Benteen, on June 25 and 26.

Documents obtained from the Little Big Horn Battlefield -- official communications, rosters and other documented sources -- indicate that the following Kentuckians (listed alphabetically) were members of the 7th cavalry:

Benjamin Brandon, a farrier who was born in Hopkinsville, killed with Custer.

First Lt. William Thomas Craycroft of Springfield, away on detached service at the time.

33

Second Lt. John Jordon Crittenden of Frankfort, killed with Custer.

Pvt. Samuel Jones Foster of Clay County, wounded on June 25 with Maj. Reno's battalion, which also saw fierce fighting.

Pvt. William M. Harris of Madison County, received the Medal of Honor for carrying water to wounded under fire in the battle of Little Big Horn.

Pvt. James Hurd of Jessamine County, with Capt. Benteen's battalion and survived. His last known address, in 1911, was Harrodsburg.

Pvt. Thomas Lawhorn of Caldwell County, not with the Army at the time of the battle.

Pvt. William D. Nugent of Grayson County, in the valley and hilltop fights with Reno's battalion.

Pvt. John Ragsdale of Hardin County, away on detached service at the Powder River, Montana Camp, at the time of the battle. He died in Dayton, Ohio, in 1942.

Pvt. Eldorado Robb of Warren County, fought with Reno's battalion.

Pvt. Richard Rollins of Breckinridge County, killed June 25 with Reno's battalion.

Pvt. Benjamin F. Rogers of Madison County, killed with Reno's battalion.

Pvt. George D. Scott of Lancaster, received the Medal of Honor for taking water to wounded under fire.

"Lonesome" Charley Reynolds, a legendary hunter, guide and scout -- whose birthplace, some historians believe, was Warren, Ill., Elizabethtown, or Stephensburg (in Hardin County) -- believed to have died with Reno while charging an Indian camp.

Pvt. Thomas W. Stevens of Madison Country, fought with Benteen's battalion.

Pvt. Thomas W. Stivers of Madison County, got the Medal of Honor for taking water to wounded under fire.

Pvt. Elijah T. Strode of Monroe County, wounded June 25 with Reno's battalion.

Pvt. William B. Whaley of Harrison County, killed with Custer.

Other native Kentuckians may have served, but their names were not located on documents available.

The names of those who died with Custer are listed on the granite marker at the battlefield near Crow Agency, Montana. The spots where they and their comrades fell are marked with small white marble slabs, scattered -- often in tiny clusters over a wide area -- on the windswept slopes overlooking the Little Big Horn River.

Cawood

January 15, 1992

Ever since Cawood Ledford disclosed that this would be his final season as the voice of the Kentucky Wildcats, I have savored each of his broadcasts all the more.

Some newcomers to the state must puzzle at the fondness of many Kentuckians for the sportscaster we call "Cawood," although most of us have never met him.

To fathom Cawood's popularity -- and in a broader sense, the state's fascination with Kentucky basketball -- one must have sat hunkered close to a 1950s-vintage radio on a winter night, fiddling with a dial knob that frequently slipped while on its journey between WHAS Radio in Louisville, WVLK in Lexington, and a host of smaller stations that carried Kentucky games.

Untold thousands of us would gather on game nights, each in his own special place, to hear coach Adolph Rupp tell Cawood once again that the Cats were not ready to play, or that Johnny Cox had not eaten well that day; that Billy Ray Lickert's ankle was bothering him, that Cotton Nash was not shooting well in practice, or that Dan Issel's knee was stiff.

Then we would listen anxiously as the Wildcats clawed their way to victory. And in their triumph, we vicariously found hope for ourselves. Regardless of our problems at the moment, we were in Kentucky, and Kentucky was the Wildcats, and they were winning. And when they were winning, then maybe in a way, so were we. Cawood was our connection. As long as he was at the game, we had tickets on the midcourt stripe.

Coal miners listened in Eastern and Western Kentucky; stablehands and thoroughbred owners listened in the Bluegrass; tobacco farmers, housewives, bankers, auto mechanics, good people and scoundrels, rich and poor, young and old, listened everywhere; in tobacco stripping rooms, milking parlors, factories and saloons. From the hills and hollows in the mountains to the backwaters of the Mississippi in Western Kentucky; from the wide places in the road to crowded cities; in mansions and in shacks, and all kinds of places in between.

Snowflakes pelted the windowpanes, wind whistled through the cracks, firelight flickered on the ceiling, coal and wood spewed and crackled in the Warm Morning stoves and open grates, and there was a wonderful glow from the old radio dial where Cawood Ledford lived.

More than one small boy or girl has peered through the cracks in the back of a tube-type radio to see if there was actually a ballgame being played inside, with Kentucky defending the goal either to the right or left of your radio dial, as Cawood would say.

Sometimes his voice sounded far away, as though he was speaking through a long cardboard cylinder. It would fade, then get loud, then fuzzy, and now and then the speaker would produce curious, whining, whirring noises that one old-timer once likened to a "cat fight."

But Cawood never stopped, and we stayed with him, step-for-step.

If all of us could have been play-by-play announcers, we'd have wanted to be like Cawood. He was a straight shooter, crisp and businesslike, and the way he strung basketball words together just sounded good-- "Topothekey -- Pulls the Trigger -- Write it Down!"

We needed no picture. Television cameras could never have done justice to the scenes that our minds were able to paint with Cawood's words.

When finally I saw Cawood's picture, he looked almost exactly as I had imagined. And when I first met him in the early 1970s, while we both worked for WHAS Radio and Television in Louisville, he was exactly as I had expected -- an all-pro, and an honest-to-goodness nice guy, to boot. At last I had a chance to thank him for all those winter nights when my Grandma Garrison and I sat beside him at the games in the light of our radio dial.

Maybe tonight, when Kentucky plays Vanderbilt, I will find an antique radio and put it near a window where the cold wind is whistling. And maybe I will pop some corn and put some logs in the fireplace to spew and crackle. Then maybe I will turn off the lamp and let firelight dance on the ceiling, and just sit and stare at the glow on the old radio dial, and listen.

And maybe, Cawood, I would not trade all of that for a season ticket on the midcourt stripe.

Fats

February 4, 1991

Sometimes when I am searching through my story files, the face of Minnesota Fats peeps out at me and I have to laugh.

It is a photograph that I took of him at Charlie Warren's Pool Room in Taylorsville, Ky., in late January 1979. I have kept the old picture, along with many others, stashed in a bulging file cabinet whose contents are of value only to me.

Until today, I have never published the picture or the story that surrounds it, and I didn't think I ever would. But each time I rifle that file drawer, Fats stares at me with an almost-grin on his face, as though he is waiting and will not give up until I make good my promise to write something about him.

As I remember it, Fats was in Louisville with a few other big-name pool players for an exhibition of some kind.

I had this off-the-wall idea that I'd like to follow him into a small-town pool room somewhere in Kentucky, unannounced, just to see what would happen when all the local pool hustlers looked up to see one of the greatest hustlers of them all shooting eight ball on the back table.

Fats loved the idea and agreed to meet me the next morning at his hotel for a trip out of town.

He was dressed in a black shirt, light slacks and a sport coat when I shook hands with him for the first time.

It amused me to hear his friends calling him "Fatty."

Fats & Paul Goodlett in Taylorsville

And although he appeared to like it, I knew that I wasn't going to call him that. Just "Fats" would do, he said.

39

He crawled into my old Ford station wagon as if he'd been ride-sharing with me all his life, and the two of us headed out of Louisville, Fats slumped on one elbow against the armrest, talking non-stop.

He said he was raised in a saloon in a rough part of New York City, and he seemed proud of it. Said he had been hustling pool since age 2, that his real name was Rudolph Wanderone and that he had picked up the name "Minnesota" when he broke all the pool players in that state at the age of 12.

I didn't buy much of that, but it didn't matter to me what he said. This was Minnesota Fats, the one Jackie Gleason immortalized in the movie "The Hustler."

Gleason was not a bad pool player himself, Fats said. He talked about Gleason and the movie, and about Las Vegas and all the "high rollers" he knew, and what a great gambler Omar Sharif was. But most of all he talked of pool hustlers he had known, and beaten, and the money he had won.

All the time, I kept thinking how much he looked and sounded like Archie Bunker (Carroll O'Connor), the leading character in the hit TV series of that day, "All in the Family."

I drove to Taylorsville, mostly because it is close to Louisville, and parked on Main Street near Charlie Warren's Pool Room.

It was getting toward noon, and I figured there would be a few pool players inside.

Fats assured me that he'd be recognized as soon as he opened the door, but I warned him that they'd not be expecting him and that he shouldn't be disappointed if no one knew him.

No sooner had we walked in and gotten our sticks off the wall than whispers began circulating, then murmuring in which his name was audible. Fats was relaxed and businesslike, but I could tell he was loving it.

"Are you Minnesota Fats?" someone asked.

Fats chuckled and smiled defiantly at me.

Then he shot a few rounds with some of the gang, as the rest of the boys gathered around to see how good he was.

To their disappointment, and mine, Fats missed a few easy ones. But with an old pool hustler, one never knows whether he is hustling or over the hill, or just saving up for one last great game.

As Fats clumsily finished a game of eight ball with a fellow named Paul Goodlett, I found myself feeling sorry for him. Everyone watched in silence.

Then, like a bolt out of the blue, the legend struck with a magnificent two-rail bank that won him the game, and we all breathed sighs of relief and congratulated him.

Fats bade the boys at Charlie's farewell, and we left the poolroom. But the old hustler was enjoying himself in small-town Kentucky, and he wasn't quite ready to leave.

"I need to stop by the bank and get some traveler's checks," he said.

It was just down the street, so we walked.

The teller who waited on Fats couldn't have been more than 23 years old.

"Do you know me?" he asked.

"I think you're Minnesota Fats," she said with a shy smile.

"Everybody knows me," Fats said as we left the bank.

Back in Louisville, I learned that a Louisville Times writer already had interviewed Fats at the hotel that morning and the story would be running that afternoon, so it was decided to kill my story.

I have seen Fats on television several times since then, shooting pool with other legends of the game, and almost never winning. It takes me back to 1979 and my old Ford wagon; the smoky warmness of Charlie Warren's Pool Room; and Fats' superb two-rail bank shot.

Two or three times a year, he looks up at me from the yellowed picture in the file drawer and yells, "Everybody knows me!"

Tom Harbut

April 28, 1993

"I found out you don't have to be a king or a queen to be a good person, and I found out that a good horse can come from anywhere," says Tom Harbut, with a photo of a Saturday Evening Post cover featuring his father William, with Man O' War.

LEXINGTON, Ky. -- Someday, Tom Harbut ought to have a front-row seat at the Kentucky Derby.

The 73-year-old Fayette County horseman has spent the better part of his life around great thoroughbreds -- and says he once even bred, raised, trained and co-owned part of a Derby horse -- but he has never been to a race at Churchill Downs.

"I always had to work," said Harbut, who was a groom for 1937 Triple Crown winner War Admiral at Lexington's Faraway Farm and later, for 30 years, a stud groom at Spendthrift Farm in Lexington, where he handled Derby winners Jet Pilot, Dark Star, Majestic Prince and other racing royalty.

Harbut's own ancestry is of some renown. His father, Will Harbut, was for many years the groom for the legendary Man O' War while the great stallion was at stud at Faraway Farm. Thousands of visitors came each year to see Man O' War and to hear Will Harbut's stories about the big red horse.

"He had a monologue similar to Johnny Carson's," Harbut said of his father. "He told the truth, but it was like cooking. You cook a good meal, but, see, you have to know how to put the right seasoning in it."

42

As Will Harbut and Man O' War grew old together, their mutual affection was widely publicized. The two appeared on the cover of the Saturday Evening Post in September 1941. Will Harbut died six years later, in the fall of 1947, at age 66; Man O' War died the next month, at age 30.

When Tom Harbut was about 10 years old, he and a friend bought a crippled foal for 50 cents, kept it for a while, then sold it for 75 cents. As a teen-ager, he broke yearlings at neighboring farms. He didn't plan to become a horseman when he returned from overseas service during World War II and took a temporary job as a groom, but the job lasted until his retirement a few years ago.

In the late 1950s, when he was making $30 a week, he paid $50 for a sickly, 2-year-old mare named Free Thought.

"I didn't have nothing to feed that horse, but I had hogs at that time and I'd go to the bakery and pick up (old) bread, so I gave her some Parkerhouse rolls, and I had some rye that you'd sow in the field, and I gave her that, and she checked up...and her coat started getting some color," Harbut said.

Before long, Free Thought was fine and Harbut and his brother-in-law, Gene Carter, who rode thoroughbreds, had the $50 mare in training in a field behind Harbut's house in the Maddox Town section of Fayette County.

"My clocker, old man Henry Tilt, sat on the porch in a rocking chair down there," Harbut recalled. "I'd say, 'Now Gene, go up there to the piggery,' where they kept the hogs, you know, 'then jog her back about middle ways of this corner up here. When you come by Henry Tilt, break her into a gallop; when you pass Frog's grocery, you have her in full gear; and when you pass those locust trees, you'll be free-wheeling. And pull up at that red gate over there.' "

Harbut finally got Free Thought to the track, and she won seven races.

But it was a colt named Touch Bar, by Nahar out of Queen O Night, that brought him closest to fame, he said. A friend had given him an old broodmare as payment for her board, and Harbut said he got permission from P.A.B. Widener of Elmendorf Farm to breed the mare to Nahar.

He wound up selling an interest in Touch Bar to a Louisiana businessman who was lucky enough at the track to get the horse into the Kentucky Derby in 1962, where he finished 11th in a field of 15 that was led by Decidedly.

His name may not have been listed as an owner of the colt on the Derby program, but Harbut said he still owned "the back wheels" at that time. He sold his interest in the horse after the Derby and used some of the money to buy his wife a car and some clothes.

"I'm the first one I know of, of any person, that has bred the horse, raised the horse, raced the horse -- and had a Kentucky Derby horse -- then sold him, right here in Maddox Town in a hog lot full of jimson weeds on two acres of ground," he said.

Someday, Tom Harbut ought to have a front-row seat at the Derby.

Old Friends

August 19, 1992

HARRODSBURG, Ky. -- I am concerned about some wonderful old friends of mine -- a rusty windmill and an aging oak tree, a two-room shack and an old black truck.

Had I seen them only once or twice, I might never have given them a second thought. But these quaint landmarks near U.S. 127 in Mercer County have weathered many seasons with me. They have smiled at me over moonlit snows when I was coming home alone late at night. They have waited for me in orange and purple sunsets on the best of days, and through blustery winds under dark, low clouds on the worst.

The windmill and the oak go back as far as I can remember, sitting off to themselves in a big field that usually is planted in corn a few miles north of Harrodsburg.

When our children were small and we passed that field on the way to their grandparents', one of them would often tap me on the shoulder and say, "Daddy, there's that windmill and tree you like."

The shack and the old black truck are a mile or so south of Harrodsburg on the same side of the road, sitting alone in the middle of a pasture under a clump of scrub hackberries.

John Steinbeck could have written a novel about the pair. I can only say that I like them.

They speak to me of dreams spent, of hardship and work and laughter. The worn-out snub-nosed truck, which has not moved since I first noticed it there years ago, must have, at one time, been covered with a hundred coats of black paint. A jimson weed grows at its left front fender.

The truck is as large as the shack, and it once was so black that it put me in mind of an interstellar black hole, or an unpainted velvet wall hanging shaped like a GMC. Only its headlights are not covered with paint, and they remind me of eyes.

Sometimes I see the shack and the truck as a comedy team, and sometimes as a sad, inseparable pair who began with nothing and finished with nothing -- except each other. The shack was there when I was a boy. The truck, a 1950s model, must have come later, but I don't remember when. Like the truck, the old shack once was covered with black paint, probably the work of the truck's owner, a barn or fence painter, I'd guess, who left the truck parked beside the shack when he went out of business.

By themselves, and away from their spots, the windmill and the old oak, the shack and the old black truck would be nothing much to look at. But chance matched them perfectly -- like rustic paintings on the countryside -- for a few of us to enjoy and appreciate.

I stopped the other day on my way home and took a picture of them, just for old time's sake.

U.S. 127 is being rebuilt and, in some areas, rerouted. When the new road is finished, it will run behind the shack and the old black truck. The windmill and the big oak will not be bypassed, but the top of the oak has died.

I wanted to pay my respects to these simple but special landmarks, and to show you their pictures, before they are gone. I owe them that much.

Time Travel

February 17, 1992

There is a little moment in time that comes back to me often: It is late afternoon on a balmy spring day in the early 1960s, and I am driving along a familiar stretch of highway in my '57 Chevy, taking a couple of my buddies home from football spring practice.

Nothing special is going on; we are all just laughing and talking and feeling like heroes. The car windows are down, and the Beach Boys are singing "Surfin' U.S.A." from WAKY Radio in Louisville, where Jumpin' Jack Sanders is guiding home "grille-grinders and radiator rammers, cruisin' down the boulevard of broken taillights."

I have thought about that flashback a lot and wondered why -- with all the better flashbacks available -- this one is frozen at that particular insignificant spot in time, as though it was some kind of benchmark event.

Maybe all the planets were in perfect alignment in those few minutes, or maybe the sweet scent of spring, mingling with the melody of the Beach Boys and the setting sun, new grass and fresh leaves just hit me in the right place to remember. And maybe the girl I had a crush on had smiled at me or touched me on the arm that day at school.

Perhaps at that moment, in that very spot, I realized that life really couldn't ever get much better for me than it was right then, riding along in that wonderful '57 Chevy, having a good time with  friends, virtually without a care in the world; all of us reeking of Old Spice or English Leather and looking no further ahead than the meals our mothers were cooking at home at that very moment.

Then again, maybe it was just that my car radio was working.

There was a spot I could hit on the dashboard, just to the left of the speaker, that would make the radio play again when it stopped. It always quit playing when a good song came on, so to be receiving the Beach Boys' latest surfing song uninterrupted was a real privilege.

Quality cruising was nearly impossible when your car radio cut out every time you crossed a speed bump at Jerry's Drive-in, or the Ranch House or the Dairy-Dip. It would have been unthinkable to thump the dashboard with a clenched fist while trying to exude coolness.

But the radio was only one of several problems that kept me from doing any serious cruising in the '57. Its passenger-door latch would sometimes stick in the open position, so that the passenger had to hold the door shut. It was inconvenient on dates.

Because of this I unwittingly developed a forerunner of what is now called a "passive restraint system," or seat belts -- a rope strung from one interior door handle to the other.

The girl who eventually became my wife once wrote a paper in college about all the idiosyncrasies of the '57, and the dates she remembered when she sat holding the passenger door closed.

Yet, for my money the designers in Detroit and Japan combined would be hard-pressed to ever come up with another car (except for a few of the 1950s model Chevys, Fords and Oldsmobiles) that had the personality of the old '57 Chevy, powered by a 283-cubic-inch V-8 with a four-barrel carburetor.

If there is anyone out there who owns a '57 Chevy hardtop -- with a radio that works -- I'll buy the gas if you'll take me for a ride late one spring afternoon to a place about 30 years back up the road.

Going Down to Dumas Walker's

April 25, 1990

MOSS, Tenn. -- Dumas Walker never planned on being a folk hero.

But fame has found him anyway. It swooped right into his 50-by-20-foot, concrete-block roadside tavern and made him a celebrity. Tune your radio to any country station in America these days and sooner or later you'll probably hear a song about him -- "Dumas Walker" -- sung by a group that calls itself "The Kentucky Headhunters.

"I told the boys that made that song I'd been famous all my life, but nobody didn't know it but me," said Walker, 74.

Dumas

"They come down here twice and had me shoot some marbles for them. They knew I used to play marbles up in there close to where they lived (some of the band members live near Edmonton, Ky.)

"They said, did I care for them making a song, and I said, 'No.' I didn't think about it coming out like it did. It's everywhere."

The Headhunters' New York manager, Mitchell Fox, says that "Dumas Walker" is ranked from No. 9 to No. 20 nationally and is still climbing, depending on which record chart is used, and that the Mercury Records album "Pickin' On Nashville," from which the hit single was released, is currently ranked No. 3.

The band is nominated for Best New Group.

Their current hit, which begins: "Let's all go . . . down to Dumas Walker's," refers to Walker as "the marble king."

Walker smiles when he hears it, remembering the marble yard he operated for years on Tenn. 52 near his package store, just below the Kentucky line.

He claims that, in their prime, he and his partner, the late Welby Lee of Tompkinsville, Ky., went undefeated in marbles for 14 years. Once, he says, they played for 40 straight days. A few years ago, on his way to a marble game in Bowling Green, Ky., Walker had a wreck and broke his arm, and he hasn't shot marbles much since.

Last December he joined The Kentucky Headhunters for the taping of their Dumas Walker music video in which he demonstrated his skill with a marble by shooting a few shots on a pool table. Most of the video was taped in the band room of Monroe County High School in Tompkinsville, using many of the school's band members and a few other local residents as extras.

The Headhunters say that Ennis' Restaurant in Greensburg, Ky., known locally as "the Greasy Spoon," also influenced the lyrics of the song, but that Dumas Walker was the primary inspiration.

As the song has grown in popularity, Walker's Package Store, which bears no markings other than a Budweiser sign and a Miller Beer thermometer next to the front door, has become something of a tourist stop.

"They was a woman here a while ago from Connecticut, wanted her picture took with me," Walker said.

He patiently signs autographs and poses for pictures -- sometimes on hands and knees on the tavern floor or parking lot -- with some of the worn marbles that have helped make him a folk hero. Sometimes his wife of 48 years, Hazel, and the couple's dog, Pepper, are asked to pose for pictures.

"That band's got a big bus with my name right over the windshield," Walker said. "They sent me a picture of it. They've been trying to take me on the road with them. But I told them I've got a dog and a woman I've got to stay with."

Secretariat

April 24, 1989

PARIS, Ky. -- Turf writers may be clamoring around Derby candidates these days, but 19-year-old Secretariat is still getting birthday and Christmas cards, cookies, peppermint candy and carrots in the mail, and drawing most of the 8,500 camera-carrying tourists to Claiborne Farm near Paris every year.

"They just want to see him and touch him," said Bobby Anderson, Claiborne's stallion foreman and Secretariat's groom. "He hit the hearts of everybody in the world, I reckon. He's probably the greatest race horse of all time.

"He has a personality all his own. He's really a smart horse," Anderson said. "He listens to your voice a lot. Most of them, you've got to kind of discipline them and make them mind, but if you raise your voice to him, you've hurt his feelings."

When Secretariat -- the 1973 Triple Crown winner and Kentucky Derby record holder -- is not grazing in the paddock where his grandfather, Nasrullah, and his father, Bold Ruler, grazed before him, he occupies his father's old stall.

The brass doorplate that bears his name and the history of the stall is polished three times a week.

"People will get straw out of his stall, take his droppings, pieces of his mane if they can get it, or whatever," Anderson said. "They keep the mane combs and the brushes cleaned out."

To get one of Secretariat's old horseshoes, you have to know someone.

Although Secretariat has a peaceful disposition, Anderson says he definitely considers himself "the king" in his paddock.

"As long as you've got him on the shank, he won't nip or grab anybody, but over that fence there he's nipped several people. Got a pierced earring out of one lady's ear," the groom recalled.

"People think they're pets, but these stallions are not just another ordinary horse."

Secretariat's only work at Claiborne Farm is breeding about 55 mares a year -- February through June. His stud fee is $40,000 -- no guarantee -- with a $40,000 bonus for a live foal.

51

So far the big red stallion -- standing slightly over 16 hands high and weighing 1,390 pounds -- has sired about 40 stakes winners and is the proud father of 1988 Preakness and Belmont winner Risen Star, 1986 Horse of the Year Lady's Secret, General Assembly and Pancho Villa, among others.

Although Claiborne Farm, a more than 3,000-acre thoroughbred empire in Bourbon County, now takes visitors only by appointment, its owners, the Hancock family, are among the few major horsemen in the Bluegrass who still welcome tourists.

And though the prized Njinsky II, Spectacular Bid, Ferdinand, Forty-Niner and Mr. Prospector are among the other famous stallions standing at Claiborne, Secretariat is usually the first horse visitors want to see.

"He's the people's horse," said Claiborne manager John Sosby. "He came along in the 1970s, right when racing needed something, and I actually think that Secretariat is to thoroughbred racing what Arnold Palmer is to golf.

"So many children -- 8-, 9- and 10-year-olds, who weren't even born when he was racing -- still want to see him. And that's quite an honor, I think."

Carolyn Hamilton, who coordinates many of Claiborne Farm's activities, says she gets dozens of cards, letters and packages each year for Secretariat from both adults and children.

"Dear Secretariat," one little girl wrote.

"How is it in the stallion barn? Who all do you know there? I wish I could meet you, but you see I don't live anywhere near Paris. ...I live in Lincoln, Nebraska.

"Please send me a picture of you. I will always remember you. I'm sending you a picture of me so you will know what I look like."

Among the other letters from fans in Florida, Louisiana, Texas, Oregon, Pennsylvania, Michigan and other states, a woman in San Rafael, Calif., wrote: "I remember the first day I saw you. It was the 4th of July, 1970, at Aqueduct. You didn't win that day, but there was something about you ... a look of pure greatness ...

"You confirmed your greatness in the Derby and Preakness, but the Belmont was a race I'll never forget. I was there, and my tears started as soon as you set your hoof on the track. You looked directly at me and nodded as if to say, 'You're going to see something special today.'

"I certainly did. I went through an entire box of tissues. ...

"Illness prevents me from visiting you in person, but I shall forever have the vision of seeing you racing with the wind. How lucky I was to be in the right place at the right time.

"Your lifelong admirer ..."

Family Trees

March 1, 1989

NOBOB, Ky. -- It is one of the little tricks that nature sometimes plays, either to amuse herself or to remind humans how little we have learned.

In a woodland in Barren County, two beech trees -- growing side by side, approximately 2 1/2 feet apart -- have been connected by a large limb.

From all appearances, the limb, which originally belonged only to the larger of the two trees, has attached itself perfectly to the smaller one. It is a curious sight -- a limb growing out of one tree and into another at a 45-degree angle.

Kentucky Division of Forestry personnel say they occasionally see some unusual tree formations, but this is a new one.

Louis Shain, a University of Kentucky forest pathologist, says he hasn't seen such a phenomenon either, but he supposes that, given the right conditions, it is possible.

"This would just be a guess, but if a branch were in close contact with another tree, and they were sufficiently sturdy that they were exerting force on one another

. . . as they rubbed against each other, you'd get the exposure of the cambium, which then would start callousing," Shain said. Cambium is the layer of cells between the wood and the bark of a tree that forms new wood and bark. "Eventually, one might grow over the other."

A good analogy, he says, would be the common occurrence of a section of barbed- or woven-wire fence being swallowed up by a tree trunk.

Beech trees being slow growers, it is nearly impossible to estimate how long it took the limb in Barren County to attach itself to another tree trunk and to heal.

Bobby Lawson, 78, a farmer whose property line runs near the trees, says some of his children brought the trees to his attention after noticing them during a walk.

Lawson recalls that, when he was a boy, there were two other beech trees in the community joined by a limb. Those trees, he says, formed "a perfect 'H.' " They have long since disappeared, and Lawson has been able to find only two people who remember them.

The larger of the recently discovered Siamese beeches is about 18 inches in diameter. The smaller is approximately 14 inches below the natural splice; above it, the smaller tree's trunk enlarges to roughly the size of its partner's.

"It looks to me like it's getting nourishment from both trees," Lawson said. "That limb just got over in there, and he rubbed into that tree some way and got started."

It is not apparent whether the two trees share a common root system. Both are about 50 feet tall and appear reasonably healthy.

They join an ever-growing list of puzzling sights, in places where nature is left to play.

Barn Clock

January 16, 1985

DANVILLE, Ky. -- Among Kentucky's many rare and charming sights is the old tower clock that, for three-quarters of a century, has so elegantly kept the time atop a rustic English barn two miles west of Danville.

For as long as most Boyle County old-timers can remember, it has been a landmark, noticed by nearly all who passed it on nearby Lebanon Pike, and heard by thousands of others for several miles around.

By all accounts, J.A. Shuttleworth, a Louisville businessman who owned the farm in the late 1800s and early 1900s, had the clock placed on the barn.

Shuttleworth is listed in records at the Filson Club in Louisville as having been president of Shuttleworth Clothing co., a wholesale clothier in Louisville, around the turn of the century.

One story has it that Shuttleworth saw the clock on a barn while visiting Austria, bought it on the spot and had it shipped to Kentucky. Another holds that he hired the maker of the Austrian clock to build one identical to the one he had seen.

In 1916, Shuttleworth sold the farm to M.T. Minor, who owned the place until his death in 1959.

The clock was operated with weights until 1956, when the L.T. Verdin Co. of Cincinnati -- reputed to be the oldest tower-clock builder in the United States -- renovated it and installed an electric motor.

The late M.C. Minor, who took over the farm after the death of his father, and whose idea it was to install the motor, told the Verdin

56

Co. that the clock had been erected in May 1910. It is presumed that the barn also was built at that time, although several large, hand-hewn logs used in its construction suggest that it could have been built earlier.

Jim Carney, who lived on the farm from 1964 to 1979, says that when the wind was right, he could hear the clock strike above the roar of a tractor while working at the back of the 313-acre farm. He used to climb into the 25-foot tower twice a year to oil the works and the motor, he said.

The bell, at least three feet in diameter, is struck by a small hammer connected to an awkward-looking, but efficient, network of cogs and rods that keep the clock running.

While M.C. Minor owned the farm, the clock's four faces were illuminated by spotlights that automatically came on at 8 p.m. and went off at midnight. Most often, according to Carney, the clock was right on time.

All through the years, tourists have stopped at the farm gate, a few hundred feet from the barn, to take snapshots of the clock and to hear its bell.

"As kids, we were up in that clock all the time," recalled Mona Thompson of Danville, the daughter of M.C. Minor. "We weren't supposed to be up there, but there were a lot of pigeons up there, and we'd go up to find the nests and see the baby pigeons.

"I had two brothers at the time, and we'd go up there and crawl out the window and slide down the barn roof. There was a lower shed down at the bottom that we'd land on, then slide down it and jump down to the ground."

The farm and its clock belonged to Mrs. Thompson and her husband, James, in 1981, when it was sold to Texas businessman Nelson Bunker Hunt, who now owns more than 9,000 acres of Central Kentucky farmland.

Buddy Edwards, co-owner of the Danville real estate firm Montgomery Associates, which sold the farm, says he used a picture and a clipping about the barn and clock from a 1974 issue of "Antiques" magazine in his sales brochure. The clock was an instant hit with the Hunts, he said.

"Mrs. Hunt particularly liked it, and I frankly think that she was significant in his purchasing the farm," Edwards said.

Sadly, the weight of the clock tower and bell have caused the barn supports to sag in recent years, and the clock no longer keeps accurate time.

But Edwards says the Hunts have expressed an interest in repairing the clock, and have asked him to find out what must be done to fix it.

With a little help, the clock may be repaired in time to fascinate a few more generations, and to count the hours through another century in the gently rolling farmland where it has become a landmark.

Rock Fence Maker

July 16, 1993

LEXINGTON, Ky. -- Edward H. Taylor has every right to be the superb stonemason that he is. The 64-year-old Fayette Countian began learning his trade nearly 50 years ago from his uncles, who had learned it in their youth from their fathers and grandfathers.

"My mother's people were all stonemasons," Taylor said. "James B. Guy -- that was my mother's uncle -- Louis Guy, Charles, John, Ed Guy -- all were brothers, all stonemasons. They had it down to an art. They helped build Keeneland Race Course and houses and stone fences all around the Bluegrass."

In 1944, when Taylor was 16, he apprenticed with the Guy brothers.

"There were a few things that they were very sensitive about," he recalled. "When they picked that rock up, they'd turn it over maybe two or three times and look at it, studying which way to hit it and how much pressure to put on it with the hammer. Oh, they hated for you to waste a rock, and if you didn't hit a rock right, you'd have some static. They'd say, 'Boy, don't hit that rock like that! You don't want nobody hittin' you like that.' They'd cuss you, too, if they got mad enough."

Their one superstition, Taylor said, was a mysterious, still-unexplained aversion to starting a job on Friday. He remembers they would often lay two or three rocks late on Thursday afternoons to avoid beginning a job the next day.

Taylor's uncles are all dead now, but several of their mortared and dry-laid rock fences remain in the Bluegrass. And their methods live on in the many fences and other structures that Taylor's hands have built over the past half-century.

"The main thing you've got to know is the grain of the rock; just like wood," he said. "You can see it, but you've got to know what you're looking for. If you go against that grain, you've lost you a rock."

Taylor once spent eight years working on a $1 million stone barn at a Bluegrass thoroughbred farm. He built a stone wall around the swimming pool at Calumet Farm and restored stonework at White Hall, the home of abolitionist Cassius Clay. Now, nearing his 65th birthday, he most enjoys smaller, more complicated jobs, building and mending rock fences and other structures that test his skill.

"When you're in restoration, you run across things that you didn't even know. Rock will teach you something every day, I don't care how good you are," he said. "Rock will fight you all the way. If it had hands, it would hit you back, I expect."

A Bluegrass tour of rock fences with Taylor is a lesson in historic fence masonry.

Some of the fences are the "two and one pattern," or the regular "running bond," or what Taylor calls the "jink" pattern.

The small flat rocks that are laid between the larger rocks in the fence are called "chinks," he said. "Eventually the ground will move, but as your ground shifts and the fence slips, these will tighten up and the fence won't go anywhere."

Even after half a century, he is still fascinated with rock fences, and he still enjoys looking at his work at the end of the day.

"I've never had a sign on my truck," he said. "Good work will keep you busy, bad work will keep you sitting. Word gets around."

On Fence Rows
May 5, 1991

One of the first things I remember my father teaching me was how to cross a woven-wire fence.

He took time explaining it -- how to climb at the post so as not to break the fence down; how to pick a post that was solid and straight; to make sure the steeples that held the wire were tight.

He showed me in some detail where to put my hands and feet, and how to avoid tearing the seat out of my pants on the strand of barbed wire across the top.

Then and there I took to fence-crossing with enthusiasm. For a person with short legs, I was good at it. I never ran into a fence I couldn't cross, until electric fences came into use.

Naturally given to exploring, and possessing a gift for piddling, I roamed the countryside near and far in the early stages of a boyhood infatuation that finally grew into a lifelong love affair with old fence rows.

They still call to me from the interstates and back roads that I travel, and it saddens me to see one bulldozed and burned.

At a distance, I know they are not pretty. But up close -- hidden in the tangle of vines, bushes, trees, weathered gray posts and rusty wire -- old fence rows are intrinsically charming and likable.

My favorites varied with the seasons.

In fall, there was a fence row where tall hickories always sprinkled the ground with nuts and pretty leaves.

In winter I was partial to a fence row that was all but hidden in a small thicket of wild cane, scattered ash and hackberry. It was crisscrossed with trails used by foxes, raccoons and other wildlife, and being there put me in mind of a place I once read about in a boy's adventure book.

Near remnants of the fence was a large hollow log -- a tree that my father, as a boy, had helped my Grandpa Crawford cut. I would sit on the log by myself sometimes, wondering how Grandpa Crawford would have liked me if he'd lived until I came along.

In spring, there was a fence row where wildflowers and moss grew beside a creek, and in summer, there were fence rows for every occasion: picking berries, catching bugs; watching groundhogs and chipmunks; listening to young quail learn to whistle 'Bob White;' and finding snakes.

The nearest I ever came to an honest-to-goodness snakebite was in a fence row one late afternoon in summer when I was about 11.

My dog snatched a large but harmless cow snake out of the fence row, and as the frightened serpent was slung past me, its open mouth somehow strafed the inside of my wrist.

I responded with my best scream of death and ran for home as the two tiny scratches turned crimson. To my disappointment, there was not much excitement over the bite, and I was no hero. I now suspect that everyone secretly thought the scratches had been self-inflicted.

Finally, no tribute to fence rows would be complete without mention of honeysuckle -- the mother of all sweet fragrances; the Chanel No. 5 of old fence rows; the whisper of everyone you've ever loved; the line in every song that made you cry; the essence of every sunset and moonrise you've ever wanted to paint.

Sometimes, when I pass an old fence row blanketed with honeysuckle, I wish I was back there just learning to cross the fence again.

Of Shakers and Brooms

July 9, 1990

SOUTH UNION, Ky. -- A small patch of broomcorn stirs in the summer breeze behind one of the stately old brick buildings on the grounds of Shaker Village at South Union on the Logan-Simpson county line.

It is reminiscent of better days at the partially restored settlement, where Shakers once owned 6,000 acres of farm land and planted about 100 acres of broomcorn to supply the broom shop -- one of 175 buildings that were once at the village.

Broom-making was a popular industry among the Shakers, who invented the flat broom and a number of other items, including the circular saw, the clothespin, the swivel foot on chairs, the water-powered washing machine and the broom press, which transformed the early brooms from round clumps of broom straw into the shape of present-day brooms.

"Everybody back then knew about Shaker brooms," said Tom Hines, director of Shaker Village. "I think they were $1.40 a dozen in the 1870s. They had a little slogan -- 'To use them once is to use them always.' "

In those days, the Shakers at South Union sold many of their brooms in New Orleans, moving them by mule and wagon to the Mississippi River, where the Shakers built flatboats to float downriver. After reaching New Orleans and selling the brooms, they dismantled the flatboats and sold the lumber.

Today Dean Watkins is the only broom maker left at South Union, and he works only part time. But he still makes brooms the old-fashioned way -- with late 19th century equipment nearly identical to that used by the Shakers.

"I watched a man here demonstrating broom-making a few years ago and got interested in it," Watkins said. "I got to looking for a machine and just about gave up. It took me two years to find one, then I had to rebuild it."

Watkins and his wife, Earlene, spend several days each year making and selling Shaker brooms at the Shaker Village Festival in June.

"You meet some interesting people," Watkins said. "Most of them want to know about broomcorn. Handling broomcorn is similar to a tobacco harvest. When the heads get full of seed, it just bends the straw every way, and you want straight straw, so you go through the field and break that head over and let it hang three or four days.

"Then you go through and cut it off, tie it in bundles, haul it in and hang it up to cure out. Then you have to strip the seeds off and sort out the length of the straws."

Watkins said it takes him about 40 minutes to make a broom, provided he is not engaged in a favorite pastime of talking with visitors about broom superstitions.

"One lady told me that when I finished sewing a broom to sweep with it a couple or three strokes before I hang it up," Watkins recalled.

"One elderly lady said that her mother always told her not to buy a broom that had over five stitches. I asked her why, and she said she didn't know.

"Another lady came in and bought a broom from me, and I remembered selling her one before that, and asked her what happened to the last one.

"She said, 'I sold my home, and I was always told that when you bring a new broom into a house, you never move it.'"

Palace of Versailles (Ky.)

June 15, 1990

VERSAILLES, Ky. -- Next to the horse farms and Rupp Arena, the Lexington Convention and Visitors Bureau says that the area's most asked-about tourist attraction is "the castle."

Since 1969, when Lexington developer Rex Martin began erecting the imposing structure to use as his residence, it has been turning the heads of nearly all who pass by it on Versailles Road, west of Keeneland Race Course, just inside the Woodford County line.

Despite the landmark's popularity, relatively little is known about it, mostly because Martin is "a very private person," as his attorney, William Jacobs of Lexington, puts it. The property is surrounded by no-trespassing signs.

The castle, complete with turrets -- which are mostly decorative -- is situated atop a hill several hundred feet north of Versailles Road. Inside its stone walls is a 10,400-square-foot stone residence with a three-car garage and six bedrooms, each with its own bath.

An open stairway from a large entry hall leads to a circular balcony on the second floor.

The house contains large rooms for a library, office, mechanical room, den, kitchen, wet bar and a powder room with a full bath. There is a 20-foot-by-50-foot swimming pool on the premises. Work on the castle, which stopped for a few years after Martin's marriage ended in divorce in the early 1970s, continues. But much of the home's interior remains unfinished.

A caretaker of the property lives in a small house nearby.

For several years attempts by reporters to contact Martin with inquiries about the castle have been unsuccessful. His last mailing address was in Crawfords, Fla. His attorney would not comment on where Martin lives.

Martin's former wife, Caroline, who got the idea for the castle design while vacationing in Europe, was quoted in a wire service article last year as saying that the house was originally supposed to have had seven bedrooms and 15 baths, including one in each of the four turrets along the wall and two for the tower cabana.

The castle property is valued at $754,000 by the Woodford County property valuation administrator's office.

"Right now I have to look upon it as a farm with a unique building on it," said Woodford PVA Jim Owen Gaines. "Rex Martin has never asked for any preferential treatment, and we have never given him any."

Gaines says that Martin shows up at the PVA office every three or four years.

"When you meet him, I assure you that you will like him," Gaines said. "He's absolutely a gentleman. He's tall and he dresses very well, and you get the feeling that you've just met a movie star."

The Needle's Eye

February 11, 1991

FRAKES, Ky. -- Perched on a jagged outcropping of rock along the crooked spine of Pine Mountain in Bell County is a geological oddity that many old-timers call "the Needle's Eye" or "the Barn Rock."

Nature has left a hole 7 or 8 feet high and about 12 feet wide in the center of a boulder, as though it has been drilled with a giant auger.

From this strange pinnacle, set in a forest of scrub timber and thickets of ivy and laurel, the nearby mountains of east Tennessee fade to a dreamy blue haze in the distance.

It is a place deserving of the legend that has, for many years, drawn people to the spot from across the country.

They come in search of a treasure that some believe was buried there 150 years ago.

As the story goes, a mysterious man named Blakely, believed to have been from North Carolina and thought by many in the community to be of Cherokee descent, moved into the area in 1932.

He lived alone and kept to himself, except for his association with a few of the local people whose services he secured to help him find natural landmarks on Pine Mountain.

A few years ago, Hodge Partin of Frakes told me that he and his father had helped "Mr. Blakely" search out markings on rocks -- some of which resembled "pony tracks" and "turkey tracks" and were still visible a few years ago in a few of the large flat rocks atop the mountain.

Partin, now 86, said then that Blakely would instruct the searchers to travel in a certain direction to find markings, which he would describe by looking at symbols on a piece of paper.

Often, Partin said, the markings were exactly where Blakely said they would be.

The Needle's Eye was among the landmarks on the map, as was a large rock in the shape of a "V" that lay below the cliff on which the Needle's Eye is located.

Partin remembered that late one day, when the "V" rock was found, Blakely said there would be a small treasure there, but that it was discovered that something had already been dug up.

Nonetheless, Blakely was convinced that a larger treasure, buried elsewhere, had not been found, and he planned to return with more tools the next morning to find it.

Blakely was so happy, Partin said, that he actually did a little dance at the Needle's Eye. "We went from there on in home, and he died before we could get home," Partin said. "I started up to my place, and him and my dad was going up the road, and directly I heard my dad holler.

"He said, 'Come here, Hodge; Mr. Blakely's fell dead!'

"I come on back down, and he was laying there in the road, dead."

Michael Paul Henson of Jeffersonville, Ind., a writer for Lost Treasure magazine, said that the late George Gibson, who was the sheriff of Bell County at the time of Blakely's death, wrote him a letter a number of years ago in which he listed the personal effects found in Blakely's cabin.

"He said that he had a bunch of books and curious papers, some of which they didn't know what to do with, and a bunch of funny-looking tools," Henson recalled. "I don't know if the tools were dowsing rods or what. And 'the paper,' he called it, was given to one of his nephews."

"The paper," of course, was the supposed map that Blakely had been using. It consisted of numerous strange symbols on the back of what appeared to be a waybill.

Some time later, Henson and a researcher in Bell County located the waybill in the possession of a member of Sheriff Gibson's family and made several copies, which have been widely circulated.

Although some symbols on the alleged map, including the Needle's Eye, are identifiable, it is not believed that anyone has deciphered the signs.

A few people in the area believe that a local family did find the treasure years ago, and that several members became wealthy as a result. It is not much talked about today.

The Needle's Eye is on private property, but the area has been searched, probably by hundreds of people, in the years since Blakely's death. A hunt is still mounted on occasion.

John Fuson, 75, of Frakes recalls spending about three days digging in a sinkhole some distance from the Needle's Eye, 45 or 50 years ago, and finding a "three-legged stool and a mallet" buried about 20 feet deep.

The searchers abandoned the dig, he said, when one wall of the hole began to cave in.

Henson believes the treasure -- if there ever was one -- might have been part of a cache left when the federal government forcibly relocated approximately 16,000 Cherokees to reservations in Oklahoma in 1838-39.

Most were allowed to take little more than they could carry on their backs and on their pack animals, he said.

Also, there were statements by Army officers at the time that the Indians had hidden much of their wealth in the Carolinas, Tennessee, Georgia and Kentucky.

Was the Needle's Eye one of those spots?

Perhaps no one will ever know.

The Oldest Postmaster

November 22, 1991

ROCKY BRANCH, Ky. -- At age 90, Edward Eli Bell is the oldest postmaster still working in the United States, four years older than the next-oldest, a woman in Ohio, the Postal Service says.

"If there's any older than I am, I'd like to see 'em," Bell said this week while sitting in the doorway of the small Rocky Branch post office in southeastern Wayne County.

Bell must often wonder whether he was postmarked by fate. His father, Charlie, named and founded the post office in 1908, and Bell practically cut his teeth on penny postcards and 2-cent stamps.

For a while, when he was a young man, he worked at a sheet-metal shop in Indianapolis making -- what else? -- mailboxes.

On Christmas Eve in 1933, he married Lona Bell, a neighbor at Rocky Branch. His father, who also operated a country grocery, soon turned the postmaster's job over to her. Bell farmed most of the 34 years that followed, but much of his daily life revolved around the post office. When his wife died in the summer of 1967, he became the postmaster.

"I guess if I hadn't quit smoking, I wouldn't be standing here talking to you right now," Bell said. "I started smoking when I was 15, but in 1982 I quit, and I've never smoked another cigarette since."

Now he hears that if he retires he will lose his zip as well as his ZIP code. So, six days a week, he's at work.

"I'm open just three hours a day now, from 8 o'clock in the morning till 11, Monday through Saturday," he said. "But I'm really open any time of day that somebody comes and wants something."

Bell and his daughter, Helen, live in a large farmhouse not far from the post office, and only a few hills north of the Tennessee border.

Bell puts the American flag out on the porch of the tiny post office every morning, and takes it back to the house at night. He generally is escorted by his trusted "guard dog," Lassie, a short-haired, overweight, mixed-breed blonde with beautiful brown eyes and a million-dollar smile, who protects the post office from squirrels.

Inside the post office, with its tongue-in-groove ceiling, vintage 1900 counter and 1945-model scales, Bell picked up the postmark stamp. He noted that, while the rubber face of the "dobber" has been replaced several times, the wooden handle is the same one his father started the post office with in 1908.

The "wanted" posters on the wall are current, and there is a big yellow-ribbon sign welcoming troops home from the Persian Gulf war. In the corner, a minnow bucket half-filled with sand serves as an ashtray; in another corner sits a 1950s dinette table and one chair.

"I've registered several boys for the draft at that table," Bell said.

There has never been much excitement at the Rocky Branch post office, and Bell and his "guard dog" like it that way. An occasional exception is when a shipment of baby chicks arrives, C.O.D.

"A lot of times the owner didn't want to take them, and I'd have to sell them for whatever I could get for them and send the money off to the company," Bell said. "People still order them. I've had two or three bunches of live chickens this year, I reckon."

Seven of Bell's postal patrons pick up their mail at the post office each day; the rest, some 65 homes, are on a rural delivery route.

Ed Bell not only remembers when the mail carriers rode horses at Rocky Branch -- one of them, he says, used to walk five miles over dirt roads delivering mail.

"We had great big wooden mailboxes back then," he said.

Bell hopes he'll be around to see a few more changes in the postal system. He has no plans to retire, and he insists that status as the oldest postmaster has not affected him.

"I don't feel no different," he said. "I'm just plain ol' Ed."

Vintage Valentines

February 13, 1991

MIDWAY, Ky. -- Happy Valentine's Day, Leroy Gummer-sheimer, wherever you are.

I don't know where you live, or even if you are living, but I have found a little sackful of your valentines from the year 1953. Judging from the handwriting on the backs, you must have been in about the third grade at the time.

Evelyn Lovell, a friend of mine who owns an antique shop in Midway, gave me all your valentines the other day, when she learned that I was in first grade in 1953. Evelyn collects antique valentines from the turn of the century. They are beautiful, ornate ones, with tender verses on them. Some of them sell for up to $300, she says. I had stopped to photograph a few of her prettiest valentines and to write a story about them.

But Leroy, your little sack of cheap valentines from 1953 took me back to the splendid days of those small heart- shaped candies with valentine greetings on them.

I liked how your classmates all spelled y o u r   n a m e   -- Gummersheimer -- differently.
"Comorhimer," one of them wrote. Then there was "leroy Gummy" and "Leroy G."

When you were in school, did everyone send each other a valentine, or did a few children in the class usually get more than the rest? Were there some who got a handful, and a few who got only one from the teacher, or a bunch of unsigned ones?

I guess, Leroy, that Valentine's Day in grade school was, for some of us, our first experience outside the playpen of how sublime and painful love and rejection could be.

Most of my valentines were, like yours, from boys, who found it far easier to send valentines to their buddies than to the girl they really liked. I don't suppose I ever sent a valentine in those days that cost more than a penny. But I searched the entire cellophane package for one with the right message for that special girl. And if I was lucky enough to get one from her, I would use every ounce of imagination at my command to draw some romantic meaning from the words.

It was no trouble finding the one from the girl who was sweet on you, Leroy. There is a folding valentine, made with better paper than the rest. On the front is a red plaid puppy smiling at a cuddly white kitten that is speckled with red hearts. The verse inside says, "Guess who thinks you're mighty nice and wants to tell you so -- Guess who likes you lots and lots -- Well, Golly! Don'tcha know? Jean."

I wonder, Leroy, where you both are now, you and Jean; whether you even know what happened to each other, and whether the valentine you got from her in 1953 would mean anything to you now. Evelyn Lovell doesn't remember where she bought the sack with your valentines inside. It was at an auction years ago, she said. Maybe it was somewhere in Missouri, but she's not sure.

Amazing, isn't it, Leroy, how the years change things.

Evelyn and I talked about it the other day, looking at some of the words of love on her 100-year-old cards. They don't make valentines like they used to, she told me, and love isn't what it used to be, either.

"Years ago, my favorite food was mashed potatoes," Evelyn recalled. "My grandmother made it with pure cream and butter. And one Thanksgiving, I go to the table and there's no mashed potatoes. And I got mad and went out on the front porch, and sat in the swing.

"My father came out and said, 'Missy, what's your problem?'

"I said, 'Grandmother knows how much I love mashed potatoes.'

"He said, in a very gentle way, 'Evelyn, reserve that word for *people*. You like mashed potatoes, you crave mashed potatoes; they're your favorite food. But you don't love them.'

"To this day, when I start to say 'I love . . .,' I hear my father say, 'No. Reserve that word.' "

Forgive me for rambling so much, Leroy, but your wrinkled sackful of valentines from 1953 so touched my tired old heart that I got to feeling, for a few minutes, as though I was back in first grade.

I could smell the oil on the pine floors, hear the steam hissing and clanging from the radiators, and see the chalk dust swirling in the air, as we all opened our brown paper sacks hanging heavy with valentines around the wall. By the way, your cards from 1953 will be here with me, if you ever want them.

Happy Valentine's Day, Leroy Gummersheimer, wherever you are.

Moonstruck
August 21, 1985

MIDDLESBORO, Ky. -- Middlesboro is the only city in the United States known to be built within a meteor crater, according to geologists.

The crater was discovered about 1960 during routine mapping by Kenneth J. Englund and John B. Roen of the U.S. Geological Survey.

Many citizens of Middlesboro still aren't aware of their town's unique location, said Rick Christopher Lasley of Middlesboro, a computer science student at Lincoln Memorial University in nearby Harrogate, Tenn.

Lasley said he learned about the crater six years ago while reading an article in the science digest, Omni, which listed Middlesboro not only as the site of one of the 15 outstanding craters in North America, but also as the most circular crater on this continent.

"I was fascinated by the story, but I only found a couple of older people here who thought they had heard about the crater, and they weren't sure," Lasley recalled.

He checked with state geologists, who confirmed the report and supplied him with maps and geological research about the crater, or meteor scar.

Lasley has since become an advocate for the crater, encouraging the governor's office to mention Middlesboro's distinction in state tourism brochures, and bringing the crater to the attention of the media.

The reason the crater has gotten so little publicity, he believes, is that it has largely been obscured by erosion and development.

Unlike the famous Barringer crater near Winslow, Ariz., which is estimated to be 22,000 years old, the Middlesboro crater has been variously estimated at 30 million to 300 million years old.

While the Barringer crater is about two-thirds of a mile in diameter, with slopes of less than 900 feet elevation, the Middlesboro crater is nearly four miles across, with slopes rising as high as 1,900 feet.

"I think the chief of interpretation at Cumberland Gap National Park described it best when he said it's like we're living in a big bowl," Lasley said. "The only way to really see it is from the air."

In an article written for the Bell County Historical Society Journal, Lasley notes that as much as 80 percent of the meteor either was blown back into the earth's atmosphere or disintegrated on impact, and that life and vegetation may have been destroyed within 50 to 100 miles.

Geological maps indicate that the center of impact occurred where the YMCA swimming pool is now on North 30th Street, and that the crater's perimeter ran through what now is the 12th Street and Cumberland Avenue intersection, he said.

Geologists believe that before the meteor hit, the area around Middlesboro may have been a wide plain, much higher than the Pinnacle overlook at 2,400 feet at Cumberland Gap.

Lasley has wondered whether Cumberland Gap itself might have been created by the impact and explosion of the meteor, but geologists say that rock formations in the area do not substantiate such a theory.

In any case, Lasley speculates, had it not been for the meteor crater, Daniel Boone and Dr. Thomas Walker, on entering Cumberland Gap, would have been faced with a high plain instead of a valley, and might well have chosen to push farther westward instead of northward into Kentucky.

Last Rites: Fletcher White

January 1, 1991

SOUTHVILLE, Ky. -- It was almost 2 o'clock, time for Fletcher White's funeral, and I was running late as usual.

I rounded a curve on Ky. 53 in southern Shelby County and was slowed by seven or eight cars and a pickup truck in front of me. My aggravation abated as I saw the holdup -- a hearse and a limousine moving unhurriedly toward the Salem Baptist Church.

Fletcher White was on his way to his own funeral.

I made "Fletch's" acquaintance about 1975 when I filmed a television story about his treasured collection of old marbles that he kept hidden in socks.

Later, after moving to Shelby County, I sometimes saw him hanging around the Kroger store or walking to a funeral. He never drove.

Funerals were important to Fletch.

He rarely missed one in Shelbyville, whether he knew the deceased or not -- sometimes attending up to three in one day -- and it seemed to hurt him when he'd go to a funeral and not many people would show up.

"That's awful, ain't it?" he would say, then launch into a story about some recent funeral that had drawn a large crowd.

My friend Whitie Gray once overheard Fletch remark that he'd sure like to go to Gene Autry's funeral -- that he bet there'd be a big crowd turn out for that one.   Fletch was a bachelor and a farmhand with a fourth-grade education, and he had no close relatives. For years he had lived with and worked for Jay and Bessie Mae Carriss, who farm and operate the Carriss grocery in Southville.

I never saw Fletch when he wasn't neatly dressed in a cap and bib overalls (or a suit for funerals) and wearing or carrying a fine-looking pair of work gloves.

Gloves were another of Fletch's favorite things, right up there with funerals and marbles.

He once told me, years ago, that he had six brand new pairs of gloves laid aside for his pallbearers to wear, and that he wanted to be laid to rest in a pair himself.

The church parking lot was full, and cars lined the highway on both sides. It was a cold, gray day, and even the aging hemlocks in the churchyard shivered in the wind.

Inside the rustic brick church, the sanctuary was warm and nearly full. Two sweet old hymns were sung by a husband and wife, and two preachers took turns speaking words of comfort and tribute about Fletcher White.

They noted that he had no close kin but that more than 300 people had visited Shannon's Funeral Home the previous night to pay their respects, not counting as many as 200 who showed up for the funeral.

"He offered us his friendship without qualification," one of the preachers said. "Many of you have provided Fletch with a ride to town, and he provided wonderful conversation along the way."

I remembered, then, how Fletch always called me "Barn," and wanted to show me his gloves; how he always asked about my dad, who he thought was Sam Crawford. I explained to him several times that I knew Sam but was not related. Fletch never got it straight, and I finally gave up and started telling him that Sam was fine.

"Fletch's memory will live far beyond his 87 years . . . in his stories and those curious gloves," the preacher was saying. "But Fletch is in a place today where gloves are not needed."

A soft beam of sunlight shone through the stained-glass window of the church sanctuary and settled about the casket where Fletch reposed in a fine navy blue suit and black dress gloves.

"He was a saint, a simple man, a work hand; the wealthiest person I know," the preacher said. "We should envy him. People did not love Fletch for his money. They did not love him for his status. They loved Fletch for who he was."

Twenty-two minutes after it began, the funeral service was over, and six pallbearers, hand-picked by Fletch White and all wearing white gloves, carried him out of the church to the cemetery.

A crowd of people followed and stood shivering in the cold, knowing it would be important to Fletch that they stayed. Then it was over and we all left, each of us taking a memory of him that now seemed somehow sweeter.

Fletch White had a wonderful funeral. One that even Gene Autry would be proud of.

Harm's Way

July 10, 1989

Fifty miles from Tucson, Ariz., 30 miles from the nearest general store and five miles down a dirt road lives noted wildlife artist Ray Harm, in a house whose only power is generated by the sun.

His name became a household word in Kentucky in the 1960s, and his limited-edition prints were among the keepsakes of the decade.

During a telephone interview recently, Harm, 61, discussed his colorful life and career, and his lasting attachment to Kentucky, which claims him as its own. He spent much of the time from the early 1960s to the mid-'70s in the state.

He was born in the Allegheny Mountains of Randolph County, W.Va., on Shavers Fork of the Cheat River.

"In my young childhood, all I did was gather herbs with my dad. Our total income was derived from digging herbs to sell to pharmaceutical people," Harm recalled. "In addition to that, he was an herb doctor ... and a sawyer in a logging camp, and he knew every daggone tree, just by looking at its bark. I guess that's where I get all my interest in the outdoors."

Harm did not stay long in West Virginia.

Although he now holds four honorary doctorates, he quit school after the sixth grade and, at 14, left home, went West and landed a job on a cattle ranch near the Wyoming-Nebraska border.

"The only thing I could draw when I was young was flies," he joked. "I didn't bathe enough."

For about six years he worked on ranches at roundup time, then followed the rodeo circuit the rest of the year -- first as a bull rider, then as a saddle and bareback bronc rider, and in his later rodeo days, as a bull-dogger and calf roper.

"I did it just for winnings on a daily basis, not to try to make the finals or anything like that," he said.

For a while, he even worked as a horse trainer for the Ringling Bros. and Barnum & Bailey Circus.

During World War II, he enlisted in the Navy and became a radio operator on a destroyer in the South Pacific.

It wasn't until after he came home that he decided to use his GI Bill benefits to go to art school -- the Cleveland Institute of Art and the Cooper School of Art, also in Cleveland. "I figured that art school would be the best thing that I could still stay outdoors and make a living at. Hell, I didn't want to go to ballet school, or machinist's school or something. Out-doors is my life."

After leaving art school about 1952, Harm remembers a nine-year struggle to get by.

"Finally I'd just given up making it on my own, so I was going to sell everything that I had to pay off my debts, and was going back to New Mexico to work as a foreman on a cattle ranch where a guy had offered me a job."

Then came a call from the late Wood Hannah, a wealthy Louisville businessman who had been at a cocktail party in Florida where the hostess had just received two of Harm's paintings.

"Hannah, who ultimately became like a father to me, commissioned me to do paintings of over 20 Kentucky birds," Harm said.

The paintings were to change Harm's life -- and the collector-print market -- forever.

Together, Hannah and Harm were the founders of the limited-edition collector-print industry.

"Copies of paintings were being made in those days, but nobody was doing *limited-edition* high-quality prints," Harm explained.

"There are several thousand artists making their living at it now, and a number of major publishing companies that radiated right out of our first one."

Ray Harm Wildlife Art Inc. soon became Frame House Gallery Publishing Co. in Louisville. And it wasn't long before collectors all over the East were calling Louisville trying to buy Ray Harm prints -- many for investment purposes.

One of his prints, the Eagle and Osprey, sold for as much as $6,000 a copy.

In 1962 Harm was commissioned to paint a family of eagles for President John Kennedy, which further fueled his celebrity.

A Louisville television station named him Kentucky's Man of the Year in 1964.

"I'm no great artist, by a long shot, and probably never will be, because I spend too much time in the field," Harm reflected. "But from a very pragmatic outlook, because I was the only one doing it in the early '60s, there kind of got to be a run on the market.

"Mr. Hannah used to say, 'When you've got something that people want ... never satisfy the demand.' That's where he came up with this limited-edition thing. We were doing 5,000 copies of each picture that I ever painted."

One exception was the Eagle and Osprey print, of which only 500 were issued at $75 each. The print currently is valued at $2,000 in collector catalogs, and Harm is now at work on Eagle and Osprey II.

He laments that, in recent years, the quality of collector art prints has declined, as some commercial illustrators have begun using sophisticated methods of tracing to make original paintings, more or less reducing the interpretive process to "paint by numbers."

Harm, who with his wife, Cathy, owns a small cattle ranch 19 miles north of the Mexican border, continues to paint the old-fashioned way -- by meticulously observing and field-sketching his wildlife subjects in their natural settings (he once spent nine weeks studying eagles on their nest) before portraying them on canvas.

Although he has been gone from Kentucky since the mid-1970s, when he and his former wife moved to Arizona for her health, he still calls the Bluegrass State home. "I don't want to lose contact with Kentucky," Harm said. "Everything successful that's ever happened to me was there."

Paintings in Words

April 29, 1985

BEATTYVILLE, Ky. -- The year was 1926. Christmas was only a few days away, and 16-year-old Nevyle Shackelford's class at Glen Eden High School in Lee County had drawn names for exchanging gifts.

"I didn't have a cent, and I decided I'd write me a story and sell it," Shackelford recalled recently. "I'd been reading about these fabulous prices that writers got, so when I came home from school that night, and after we'd eaten supper and everybody had gone to bed, I laid down in front of the grate and took a sheet of pulpwood paper and a pencil and wrote a story."

He sent it to a magazine called Open Road For Boys, and within a few days, he received a check for $6.

"That ruined me," said Shackelford, now 75, a veteran writer, naturalist and member of the Kentucky Journalism Hall of Fame.

Fortunately for his readers, Shackelford, or "Shack" as many of his friends call him, has never stopped writing. There is a charm in his style that ensures that his work will be forever young, such as a piece he wrote in 1970:

"Down below my old boyhood home, high upon the North Fork River, there was a low, mossy cliff with a spring of clear, cold everlasting water beneath. On top of this cliff was an aged beech upon whose scarred trunk numerous persons in times gone by, in an instinctive outreaching for some small measure of immortality and a hope of perpetuating a knowledge of their existence upon a forgetful earth, had carved their initials.

"Every spring I used to make a pilgrimage to this spot to read the inscriptions carved upon this tree trunk, but more to smell again the unforgettable fragrance of the trailing arbutus that flourished under the beech in the acid soil of the clifftop. There's nothing this side of Heaven which smells sweeter than the tiny pinkish flower of this woodland vine, and it therefore is undoubtedly divine in origin, for truly it could hardly have happened by chance."

Those lines are from a section on trailing arbutus in a 62-page booklet, Wildflowers of Kentucky, Written by Shackelford for use by the University of Kentucky College or Agriculture Cooperative Extension Service.

83

He is a mountain man, modest and plainspoken, who has learned more of nature in the backwoods than in a library. Although he describes himself as an "ordinary journalist," one gets the impression that Shackelford might have felt quite at home with Thoreau at Walden Pond.

"I never remember when I didn't want to write, and I have had a lifelong interest in plants," he reflected. "My mother said when I was a baby, before I could talk, she'd carry me in her arms when she'd go to milk of a night, and every wildflower that I saw, I'd want to know what it was."

In his younger days, Shackelford taught school, but writing was his first love. While teaching, he sold articles to Progressive Farmer, Farm and Ranch, Country Gentleman, Grit and numerous other publications.

"I'd get a dollar, two dollars, three, sometimes four, and I went on for several years doing that. I even wrote Christmas card jingles," Shackelford recalled with a laugh. "My crowning glory was when I had a picture published in Life magazine. It was a picture of an old circuit rider, and they paid me $10 for it."

After military service, Shackelford found a job with the Kentucky Post. He later worked as a reporter for the Lexington Herald and as a stringer for two major wire services and a Knoxville, Tenn., paper, before joining the University of Kentucky as an information writer in 1955.

It was during his 20 years at the university that Shackelford's talent for nature writing blossomed. His columns on outdoor lore, farming and nostalgia appeared in newspapers and periodicals statewide, and were even requested by universities and news organizations in other states.

While some writers use words to tell stories, others use them to paint pictures. Shackelford is of the latter order.

"Through the milk gap, an old road, which once knew the footsteps of pioneers, skirted the hillside, dipped down, crossed a small creek, now muted in the languor of summer, made a sharp turn, and then led off through a dense stand of second growth timber," one of his tales began.

"It was late July and I took this old thoroughfare with a feeling of elation and a spirit of adventure, because no one ever knows what he may find on such a little-used trail when the season is high and the country wide."

Nevyle Shackelford -- an ordinary journalist who writes extraordinarily well.

Milkweed Pods and Peach Pits

September 20, 1989

Today we take up the subjects of milkweed pods and peach pits.

For the few who may wish to read on, allow me to explain that I occasionally write something just for the record, even if the subjects may seem dull and un-newsworthy.

I apologize to those bored by such trivia, but there is much insignifica worth remembering that often is overlooked or ignored by writers.

I have always tried to sprinkle enough such material through my work that someone who would appreciate it might still be able to find it 50 to 75 years from now in a dehydrated clipping that had miraculously escaped the trash can.

So it is with milkweed pods and peach pits.

Milkweeds are generally plentiful in pastures and fence rows over much of Kentucky and surrounding states, although I have noticed that they do appear to favor some spots over others.

Toward the end of summer, the milkweed's purplish flowers form pods that eventually burst open and send silken tufts into the wind, each carrying a seed surrounded by a corklike substance that keeps them afloat in water.

I had never thought of the milkweed as more interesting than other weeds until Jim Bryson, a storekeeper on Shultz Creek in Greenup County, told me a few years back that he recalled that milkweed pods were once gathered for use in making life jackets.

Then another of my Greenup County friends, outdoor writer and photographer Soc Clay, remembered gathering them.

It was during World War II, he said, when he was a student at the one-room Biggs Elementary School in Greenup County. The collection drive for milkweed pods was similar to the more publicized wartime drive for scrap iron.

Children would bring in milkweed pods by the sack and would empty them into a big bin in the back of the room.

Clay never knew what, if anything, the school was paid for the milkweed pods, or who took delivery of them. But he believes the school got at least enough to buy refreshments for a party that capped off the patriotic effort.

Curators at the Navy Museum in Washington and at a few other military museums around the country found the milkweed story interesting but were unable to confirm it.

However the World Book Encyclopedia, in a a one-line mention of the subject in its 1959 edition, states, "In 1942 milkweed floss was collected as a wartime substitute for the kapok fiber used in life belts."

Lacking further information, we are left to guess as to how and where the life jackets were made, and whether the contents of the milkweed pod proved a fitting substitute for kapok -- a fiber obtained from the fruit of the silk-cotton tree of Malaysia.

Several Kentuckians in various parts of the state who were asked about milkweed collecting vaguely recalled the effort but could not remember particulars.

Norman Lawson, assistant statute reviser for the Kentucky Legislative Research Commission, could not add to the milkweed story, but he did remember reading, in William D. Murray's 1937 "History of the Boy Scouts of America," that during World War I the Boy Scouts helped the War Department collect peach pits and nutshells for use in making carbon for gas masks.

The history states that the Scouts' house-to-house canvass collected 100 railroad carloads of fruit pits.

Further, it tells of how President Woodrow Wilson enlisted the Scouts' help in conducting a nationwide census of black walnut trees.

Because black walnut was used in gun stocks and airplane propellers, it was referred to in those days as the "Liberty Tree." Scouts located and reported a total of about 21 million board feet of black walnut.

Fill 'Er Up

August 23, 1991

HOPKINSVILLE, Ky. -- Maybe it was the drowsy glow of the Western Kentucky sunset behind the abandoned filling station that made me turn around and go back. Or it could've been the skeletons of two 1950s-vintage gasoline pumps out front.

I have passed the place many times over the years, on trips between Hopkinsville and Fort Campbell, but never had it looked so inviting.

An honest-to-goodness filling station. How refreshingly quaint these days. Two gas pumps -- a red and a silver one. There were only two decisions in those days -- regular or ethyl. No telephones to operate, no speakers, no numbered pumps, no digital readouts, no buttons to push for cash or credit card, no blends or additives with fancy names to figure out.

"Filling station." It seemed years since I had heard that name, and I said it aloud to hear how it sounded -- to savor its simplicity. Then I reached for my camera and got out to take some pictures.

I suppose filling stations were the parents of the now-endangered service stations, and the grandparents of the funky, Johnny-come-lately super convenience stations, with pump islands that talk.

Weeds were growing now around the pumps of this boarded-up station which rang up its last sale many years ago. Its small parking area was still covered with white gravel, no blacktop. The price per gallon on the red pump was still set at 29.9 cents for regular.

I guessed it was a Texaco station back in the 1940s and '50s, but the two big firemen's hats that I remembered having been on the pumps were gone, and so was the Texaco star that must have stood out front.

There was a lonely charm about the place, so quiet now that if I had listened closely, I'm sure I could have heard the echoes of "fill 'er up," the hum of the pumps, the ringing of the bell and maybe even the squirts from the pump spray bottles that were used for cleaning windshields back then.

Self-service was unheard of in those days, and if you saw someone other than a station employee pumping gas, you could pretty well figure he was a trusted friend of the attendant.

Just as I finished snapping a few pictures, a state trooper pulled in behind me, looked me over good, and asked, "Is there something special about those gas pumps?"

"No," I said, "I just wanted to look at them for a minute. I remember how I used to like watching that little propeller spin in that glass bulb full of gasoline on the side of the pump (sometimes the propeller blades were different colors), and how I liked to hear the bell ring as the gallons clicked off."

The trooper smiled. The old filling station had been sitting there, empty, he said, the 20 years since he'd been working that stretch of road, and he figured it had shut down long before that. He had often wondered about the place himself.

A few days earlier, he had been to an auction where an antique gasoline pump had sold. It had a five-gallon glass canister at the top and a handle that was used to pump the canister full of fuel before it was drained through a hose into the car's tank.

"I hate to admit this," I said, "and I know now that it was dangerous. But when I was a kid, I loved the smell of gasoline, and sometimes before my dad put the gas cap back on, I would try to get my nose close enough to the gas tank for a few good whiffs."

"Yeah," the trooper said, smiling again as he started his car and pulled away. "I used to like to smell it myself."

Floyd's Barber Shop

September 18, 1992

Floyd's Barber Shop in downtown Mount Airy, N.C. -- where actor Andy Griffith got haircuts as a young man and which he immortalized in "The Andy Griffith Show" -- is installing two antique barber chairs from Louisville.

Owner Russell Hiatt, 68, who has been barbering for 46 years and who cut Griffith's hair a few times in their younger days, drove to Louisville yesterday to get the two chairs, which Joe Rowland removed from his shop when he closed it and started working as a letter carrier about 1960.

Rowland, 65, said discussions about the chairs began when he and his wife, Eva, stopped in

Rowland and Hiatt
in Rowland's garage

Mount Airy several weeks ago on their way back from a vacation at North Carolina's Outer Banks.

Among the surprisingly few Andy Griffith-related tourist attractions in the small town near the Virginia border is Floyd's Barber Shop on Main, next door to the Snappy Lunch, a cafe that is mentioned in several episodes of the 1960s television series, which is still a favorite in syndication.

"When I went in the barber shop, of course I wanted to establish a rapport with Russell, so I told him I was a barber and still had a license, and we talked for a while," Rowland said. "He even let me cut one customer's hair while he was talking to somebody."

During the conversation, Hiatt mentioned that his business had outgrown its two chairs and that he needed a third chair, but didn't know where he'd ever find an old chair to match the decor.

Rowland mentioned the two chairs in his garage. Hiatt was interested. Rowland said he'd been offered $300 apiece. Hiatt said he'd take them at that price. Rowland said he'd think about it.

"On the way home, Eva and I talked about it, and we stopped at Frankfort to see our son who lives there, and he said, 'Dad, you don't need those old barber chairs. Put a little plate on them with your name on it and give them to the man.' So I did that. I really look forward to our three boys and grandchildren walking in and seeing their grandpa's barber chairs in Floyd's Barber Shop in Mayberry," the fictional setting of the TV show, Rowland said.

Yesterday morning, Hiatt and a friend, Ralph Dollyhigh, drove to Louisville in a pickup truck and took the chairs back to Floyd's.

But first, over strawberry cobbler and coffee at the Rowlands', they rehashed tales of bygone days at the shop, and everyday life in the town that became TV's beloved Mayberry.

"When I started there it was called the City Barber Shop. Andy Griffith was in college at the University of North Carolina then, but he would come home on breaks and was there during the summer," recalled Hiatt, who is often called "Floyd" by tourists.

"He was sitting there one day with those feet sticking way out in the floor -- laying back, you know -- and I just had gone to work. Everybody was busy but me. 'Well,' he said, 'you might as well cut my hair. You've got to learn on somebody.' That was the first time I ever cut his hair. And I cut it once or twice more after that."

After Griffith went to Hollywood, he rarely returned to Mount Airy, Hiatt said. The actors who portrayed Otis Campbell and Helen Crump have visited the barber shop, but Hiatt said he never met Howard McNear, the man who played Floyd Lawson, the barber.

Hiatt is amazed by the number of tourists who come to his shop -- about 900 one month this summer -- to talk about "The Andy Griffith Show" and to buy souvenir caps, T-shirts and mugs that say "Floyd's Barber Shop . . . Two Chairs, No Waiting."

Soon, there will be four chairs -- including a big one and a child's chair, both gifts, from Joe Rowland's Barber Shop in Louisville.

Buttercups

March 14, 1990

Some call them jonquils or daffodils. I call them buttercups.

Technically, I know I'm wrong. The real buttercup is a wildflower, a cousin of the larkspur. But I have spent my life calling jonquils buttercups -- in the mistaken way that people often choose to call things what they'd *like* them to be -- and it would feel awkward for me to change at this late date only for the sake of seeming knowledgeable.

Buttercups love to grow where old houses have stood.

It is almost as though they consider it their duty every spring to mark such spots with beautiful flowers to remind us of where we have been and what we left there.

In a place very dear to my family, a little sea of buttercups appears each spring to greet us on some balmy afternoon when we are drawn to the site of "the old home place."

I suspect that our homing instinct must be akin to that of birds and butter-flies, inexplicably pulled back each year to where they are supposed to be at precisely the right time.

My folks picking buttercups

For my family, that is the old home place when the buttercups bloom.

Some buttercups are the yellow of country butter; others more resemble margarine. They are not very high in the social order of flowers, but I love them for sentimental reasons.

The buttercup speaks to me of faraway days of youth; of sweet springs that I remember and sounds that came to me when my ears were new: gurgles and murmurings, the cackling of a wood-hen hidden in the tall sycamores, spring peepers in full chorus, and the bleating of spring lambs, calling for their mothers in distant pastures at twilight.

I see, in a patch of buttercups, the best of my past -- my mother guiding me toward a clump of yellow blooms in search of Easter eggs; my dad, a cane fishing pole in his hand, wading through the buttercups with me on the way to Hanging Fork Creek; my children's dimpled hands, reaching to pick their first flower -- a buttercup.

There are sad, fleeting thoughts of grandparents who once walked among these flowers. Grandmothers, you know, always brag on the crumpled, wilted buttercup bouquets that are brought to them in little hands.

Where the old home place once stood is now a thicket of black locusts. There is still a faint, grassed-over remnant of the old creek road nearby, and, across the way, the crumbling stone face of the well house.

Everything is old here now, except the buttercups, delicate survivors, dancing in the warm breeze, as fresh and new as they looked when I scampered barefoot through them as a child.

How is it that these most fragile little ornaments of nature remain so durable and ageless through the generations of floods, droughts and icy winters, while all else vanishes so soon?

Like people and other creatures of nature, have these flowers a need to return each year to this place where they belong?

Do they know that we come here every spring to see them, and that they sometimes make us feel better about growing older?

I wonder if they call themselves jonquils or daffodils. And do they laugh, when I am gone, because I call them buttercups?

Fractured Reflections

October 3, 1986

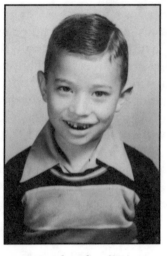

It is that time of year again -- school picture day.

When I was in school, the announcement was never made far in advance, but even when it was, there were always a few of us who nature, in its cruelty, left woefully unprepared for the camera.

One of my front teeth was missing for my first-grade picture, but my mother gave my face and ears a particularly hard scrubbing that morning, before parting the sea of Vaseline Hair Tonic on my head with a comb whose teeth felt as though they were made of nails.

She asked how I planned to look when my picture was taken. I smiled from ear to ear, and I think she gave me a sympathetic smile and a hug.

I was shaking when our class lined up for pictures, and we all waited nervously as, one by one, each first-grader disappeared behind a dark partition and a brilliant flash of light burst forth.

Most of us were unaccustomed to having our pictures taken, and school pictures were of some importance.

Finally, it was my turn behind the partition. The photographer lifted my chin, peeped from behind the camera, made a funny face, and I responded with my big smile. Poof! Another adorable face was immortalized for the school yearbook.

I was never nervous about school pictures after that, but the older I got, the worse my pictures became.

At first, I noticed that classmates were reluctant to exchange pictures with me, but I did not realize the severity of my problem until my freshman year in high school, when even my mother did not want one.

94

In desperation, I turned to my buddies, Darrell Barrett, Gary Bastin, Gary Kendrick and Ronnie Young, who were also having trouble getting rid of their school pictures.

Senior year at Stanford High School offered a last chance for a school picture I could be proud of, but to quote Dan Rather, "the camera never blinks."

I was nearly hidden on the back row in the football team photo and, in the individual player photos, I had to wear my high-topped football cleats, a disgrace for any running back.

Footwear continued to plague me when, one afternoon, I was called away from marking the football field with lime to have my picture made with the Future Homemakers, whose members had elected me chapter sweetheart after I helped them move some heavy appliances.

There I was, sitting between two pretty girls, club officers Pat McCauley and Sheila Seaman, wearing a pair of discarded tennis shoes -- with the toes out -- that I had found in the locker room. I was forced to move more heavy appliances to keep my sweetheartship from being revoked.

Just before the senior class pictures were taken, I received a nasty scrape on the side of my face during a football game.

I was elated.

During every game I had hoped for a visible cut or bruise to prove that I had seen some tough grid-iron action. What luck to have sustained the hideous abrasion on my face just before the senior class pictures were made, thereby preserving for future generations that would see the yearbook evidence that I had shed blood in the Wildcats' quest for victory.

But, alas, when the pictures returned, the photographer had airbrushed the scrape.

To this day, I display only one of my school pictures in the family photo album -- the one made in the first grade.

It is wrapped in plastic and kept away from the other pictures. Not because it is valuable, but because every year, about school picture day, it oozes an oily substance that smells like Vaseline Hair Tonic.

Life After Football

October 15, 1990

SHELBYVILLE, Ky. -- The first girl in Kentucky to score in a high school football game has settled into a quiet career of teaching algebra and coaching girls' basketball.

Beth Bates, who in 1982 and '83 kicked her way into high school sports history in Kentucky and Tennessee by becoming the first girl to score in each state, says that most of her students at Shelby County West Middle School probably don't know about her gridiron past.

"I felt that they needed to get to know me as a teacher before they knew anything else about me," she said. "I'm very proud of what I did . . . but I don't want to make a big deal out of it."

In addition to being a star forward for the Williamsburg High School girls' basketball team, Bates was a place kicker for the school's football team her junior and senior years, booting a total of nine points and earning the affectionate nickname "Super Shoe" from her fellow Yellowjacket players and the student body.

Sports Illustrated, the Los Angeles Times and other national and regional media took notice of her kicking, but Bates reacted modestly to the accolades.

"With my situation, it was something that worked out," she explained. "I don't feel that I'm any better athletically than a lot of other people, but it was the right time and the right place.

"I had my brother (who played quarterback) there. It was a small school, and I lived close to school and could practice on my own, and the coach asked me to play."

Williamsburg football coach Bob Rose said in a 1982 interview that Bates got his attention when she won two punt, pass and kick competitions against boys -- in the fourth and sixth grades. She was also a high draft pick to quarterback the sandlot football games that the boys played at recess, he said.

"I'm sure there are girl soccer players who can kick the ball farther than I did," Bates said. "It was just a situation where I was willing to work at it . . . and since we didn't have any other sports for girls besides basketball at the time, I didn't have anything else to do."

Bates hung up her cleats and shoulder pads after high school to become a point guard at Belmont College in Nashville, Tenn.

She was an assistant coach of the women's team at the college for one season before moving to Shelby County to become a teacher in the fall of 1989.

Over the years, she has been asked numerous times for her opinion of girls playing high school football.

"I had to really do a lot of soul-searching about it," she said last week. "I feel that up until boys start getting their growth spurt, girls can compete with them. But as they get older -- especially on the junior and senior level -- in my case, I didn't feel like I was physically capable of competing, strengthwise.

"I don't know if it's because I'm getting older, but when I watch college and professional football and watch them getting hit, I just don't see how those bodies can withstand that type of hitting," Bates added.

"I've hardly touched a football since high school," she said. "Golf is my big game now."

Toe-to-Toe With Joe Louis

August 5, 1987

SHELBYVILLE, Ky. -- There aren't many men at Shelby Manor Nursing Home -- or anywhere else -- who can tell of stepping into the ring against Joe Louis when Louis was the world heavyweight boxing champion.

Claude Brown, 69, of Shelby County remembers it far more vividly than he'd like to admit.

"What got me started boxing was reading a magazine one time where Jack Dempsey made $750,000 in 3 minutes and 50 seconds," Brown recalled.

"Footsie" Brown, as folks around the farming community of Cropper knew him, was 19 then, wearing a size 12 EE shoe.

"We used to have two anvils over there -- one was 77 pounds, the other 103 pounds. I could raise that 77-pound one with either hand, and I could lift that 103-pound one with my right hand," Brown said.

On July 1, 1942, a few months after Joe Louis had been ordered to report for induction into the Army at Chicago, Brown was also drafted.

Later that year, Brown, who stood 5-foot-11 and weighed about 200 pounds, won a boxing championship at Fort Bragg, N.C., then lost a close decision for the championship of Camp McCoy, Wis.

His outfit was sent to North Africa at the end of 1942, and Brown continued boxing, winning the inter-allied professional heavyweight championship in Algiers with a second-round knockout and the professional heavyweight title of Armed Forces in the Mediterranean.

It was in July 1944 that Brown finally experienced what every heavyweight of his day must have dreamed of -- a chance to put the gloves on with the "Brown Bomber" himself, heavyweight champion Joe Louis.

The champ, who had beaten the likes of Max Baer, Max Schmeling, Jimmy Braddock and Billy Conn agreed to fight two rounds each with Brown and with Chicago's Eddie "Kid" Perry in a stadium in Oran, Africa. Brown was first.

"He made it pretty rough on me for an exhibition match," the Kentuckian said of Louis. "Of course, I was coming in there with him, you know, pretty good. I opened up on him pretty well at times . . . and it seemed like he opened up pretty well on me at times, too.

"I knew I could give him a good punch, but it seemed like the harder I hit him, the harder he hit me back. He was pretty much in his prime then, you know."

Although a newspaper clipping detailing the bout said that Louis "took it easy" on Brown and Kid Perry, the same clipping detailed what must have been the exchange of punches that Brown referred to when he said "the harder I hit him, the harder he hit me back."

"Brown caught a dandy on the jaw in the first that had him momentarily staggered and blinking," the news account said. "In the second, he stayed with Joe in a fast exchange of body punches, all of which were kept in check by the champ.

"At the finish of their rounds, both Brown and Perry were breathing hard, while Joe was as cool as a cucumber, without a glint of sweat on him."

Brown apparently enjoyed mixing it up with big-name fighters, for he agreed to a three-round exhibition bout in France a few months later with Billy Conn, who had nearly beaten Louis for the championship just before the war broke out.

Brown thought he beat Conn in the exhibition, and he correctly predicted in a Buffalo, N.Y., newspaper that Louis would stop Conn easily in the 1946 rematch, which ended when Conn was knocked out after eight uneventful rounds.

"My last fight? I guess it was several years ago," Brown said, sitting on the edge of his bed at the nursing home. "It's hard to believe that I'm that old now, 69. Seems like I've lost my sight in this eye, and my feet and legs are bothering me a lot."

After military service -- during which newspaper clippings indicate that Brown compiled a record of 20 wins, 7 losses and 1 draw -- he had a few professional bouts as a civilian and even tried wrestling, without much success.

"I think $600 is the most I ever made out of a fight," he said.

In later life he worked at a packing house in Louisville, and he has lived the last several years back where it all began, in the little community of Cropper, where he once read stories about Jack Dempsey and lifted anvils with one hand.

A Tarnished Memory

June 24, 1992

PAINT LICK, Ky. -- The International Olympic Committee would like Kentuckian Kenny Davis to pick up a silver medal that has been waiting for him in a vault in Switzerland since the 1972 Summer Olympics. The committee may as well forget it.

"I definitely don't want it," said Davis, who disclosed in the June issue of Sports Illustrated that he has specified in his will that his family and descendants are never to accept the medal. Silver medals were awarded to him and to the other 11 members of the 1972 U.S. Olympic basketball team, which lost to the U.S.S.R. in a bizarre six-second finish in the final game of the Olympics in Munich, West Germany.

Davis, a Wayne County High School all-stater and three-time All-America guard who still holds the career scoring record at Georgetown College, was drafted by the New York Knicks of the NBA and the Carolina Cougars of the old ABA in 1971. But he passed up tryouts because his goal was to make the Olympic team.

Sixty-seven players were invited to try out for the 12 spots.

"Out of 12 players, I was probably the 12th man on the team," said Davis, the only member of the team from a small college and, at 6-foot-1, the smallest player on the squad. "Of course, that's kind of like going to heaven; as long as you make it..."

During an interview this week at the 130-acre farm in Garrard County where he lives with his wife, Rita, and their teen-age son and daughter, Bryan and Jill, the 43-year-old Davis -- now a sales representative for Converse athletic shoes -- recounted the incredible and devastating series of events in that 1972 game.

101

With only six seconds left and the United States trailing the Soviets 49-48, Doug Collins stripped the ball from a Soviet player, went in for a layup and was nearly knocked out by a Soviet player. Collins sank both free throws to put the United States ahead by one with three seconds remaining.

Prohibited by international rules from calling a timeout after free throws, the Soviets inbounded the ball. But instead of then pushing the button to call a timeout -- as was required -- the Soviet coach and most of the bench spilled onto the court, in violation, demanding that the clock be stopped.

Davis agrees with Sports Illustrated's chronology of what happened next -- of the referee's stopping the clock at one second because there were "fans" on the court and disallowing a Soviet timeout.

"The Soviets inbound again; the passer steps on the line, but no call is made. His long pass is deflected. The buzzer sounds. The Americans go wild, 50-49 winners of the gold."

Then, from out of the stands stepped R. William Jones of Great Britain, an official of the International Amateur Basketball Federation who -- without authority to do so -- overruled the floor officials, granted the Soviets a timeout and ordered that three seconds be put back on the clock.

As the Soviets lined up to inbound, a referee, citing a non-existent rule in international play, ordered U.S. player Tom McMillen to back off the inbound passer or be hit with a technical foul.

There was a length-of-the-court pass, and a Soviet player leaped, grabbed the ball and made the basket to give the Soviets a 51-50 victory and a tainted gold medal.

The U.S. team did not show up at the award ceremony to accept the silver.

Davis, who found himself fitting the 1976 Soviet basketball team with Converse athletic shoes for the Olympics in Montreal, says he holds no animosity toward the '72 Soviet team.

"Some of the same players, I think eight out of the 12, were on that team. I couldn't communicate that much with them...but they knew who I was," said Davis. "I think deep down they have a lot of pride, too, and they knew that they did not win legitimately."

Every few years members of the 1972 U.S. Olympic basketball team get a letter from USA Basketball asking if they want the silver medal. It stipulates that the decision must be unanimous.

Sports Illustrated notes that 10 of the 12 players still say they vote no. Would Kenny Davis vote no even if the 11 others voted to accept the silver medal?

"I wouldn't want to prevent them from getting it," he said. "But if it is a unanimous decision that they have to have, then I would not give them that, because I personally do not want mine....I still would vote no."

"Mac" Kilduff Remembers J.F.K.

November 20, 1992

BEATTYVILLE, Ky. -- The man who announced to the world the death of President John F. Kennedy on Nov. 22, 1963, and who rode two cars behind the president's limousine in the Dallas motorcade, said it was several years before he could bring himself to discuss the details of that awful afternoon.

Former White House deputy press secretary Malcolm M. "Mac" Kilduff, 65, now a lecturer and writer, has lived in Beattyville since 1977. His wife, Rosemary, a Beattyville native who for many years was a staffer for Sens. Earle Clements of Kentucky, Vance Hartke of Indiana and Hubert Humphrey of Minnesota, now writes for the Beattyville Enterprise.

On the day of the assassination, Kilduff had accompanied President Kennedy and his wife, Jackie, to Dallas-Fort Worth aboard Air Force One on what was to have been a routine assignment, coordinating news coverage of the visit.

Normally, Press Secretary Pierre Salinger would have handled the responsibilities, but Salinger was in Japan that week.

Kilduff was riding with several reporters two cars behind the president. He remembers seeing a Hertz billboard atop the Texas School Book Depository and asking someone, "What the hell is a school book depository?" seconds before he heard what he thought was a firecracker. Not until he saw the commotion among Secret Service agents around the president's car did he realize something was wrong, and even then he put aside thoughts of the worst.

"Even when we got to Parkland Hospital, it was inconceivable to me. I thought, 'The president's not dead, obviously ... this is America.' "

104

Minutes later, Kilduff would scribble a simple statement in
longhand, which he read to reporters waiting in a makeshift press
room.

" 'President John F. Kennedy was killed by a gunshot wound in
the brain, here in Dallas today'...I could not bring myself to say those
words, at first, because that would make it real," Kilduff said.

Prior to the
announcement,
Kilduff had broken
the news of the
president's death to
Lyndon and Lady
Bird Johnson.

"Lady Bird kind
of screamed,"
Kilduff remembers,
"and Johnson's
immediate reaction
was, 'We don't know
what kind of a com-
munist conspiracy this might be. I think I'd better get back to Air
Force One.' "

Later that afternoon, Kilduff helped load Kennedy's coffin aboard
Air Force One. Lyndon Johnson took the oath as president in a
tearful, grim ceremony aboard the plane soon afterward.

Kilduff asked Jackie Kennedy, who was with the coffin in the rear
of the plane, if she wanted to come forward for the swearing-in.

"She said, yes, she would come forward, and I looked down and
her hands and all under her watch were just covered with blood,"
Kilduff recalled. "I asked if she wanted to clean up first, and her
answer was rather strange. She said, 'No, let them see what they've
done.' "

Kilduff is convinced that there was no conspiracy to kill Kennedy;
that Lee Harvey Oswald acted alone, and that Oswald's target was
not Kennedy, but Texas Gov. John Connally who, as secretary of the
Navy, had approved the court-martial of Oswald and his subsequent
discharge from the U.S. Marine Corps. Connally was critically
wounded, but survived.

Kilduff believes that the angle of the line of fire and the fact that the president's limousine speeded up suddenly at that point in the motorcade route may account for why the bullets struck Kennedy, who was seated behind Connally.

A few days before the trip to Dallas, after Kennedy laid a wreath at the Tomb of the Unknown Soldier in Arlington Cemetery, Kilduff said the president quietly called him aside and gave him a second wreath -- to be placed at the grave of Kilduff's 4 1/2-year-old son, Kevin, who had drowned in June 1961, and who is buried in Arlington.

At Kennedy's funeral two weeks later, Kilduff contained his grief until the "missing man" formation of military fighter planes passed low overhead, followed by Air Force One, which dipped its wing to the fallen president and climbed skyward at full throttle.

Then Kilduff cried.

On Secret Pond

January 3, 1990

STANFORD, Ky. -- For nearly 30 years I have carried -- in my mind -- a picture of a place that I used to visit as a boy.

To the few others who saw it, I suppose it was nothing special. Just an old pond in an out-of-the-way place, surrounded by decrepit trees and tangled bushes. But I loved to go there, for the pond cast upon me an inexplicable spell.

When I first saw it, late one winter day at age 11 or 12, I was spending most of my spare time exploring the woods and meadows that lay beyond the familiar fence rows, thickets and pastures that were my native range.

The pond, cradled in a low place in a rolling field well away from everything, peeped at me through the spitting snow and the trees that encircled it, and a family of wild mallards waited until I moved closer before lifting into the winter sky.

I froze the scene in my mind and, at that moment, adopted the pond as my secret place. I never fished or hunted there; never went there with anyone else; never remember uttering a word there. Usually, I stood or sat at a distance from the pond, just looking at it, and liking it.

There was a peaceful, soothing atmosphere about the spot, enhanced by its obscurity and by my memories of that enchanted first visit in the snow.

It was a good distance from our place and I was not sure who owned the large farm on which it was located, knowing only that its owners lived far away, and that the pond was -- in the cosmic scheme of things -- more mine than theirs.

I have thought about the place several times over the years since I moved away, and in recent weeks I had wondered if it was still there.

So in mid-afternoon on New Year's Eve, I decided to find out.

I drove 70 miles to Lincoln County and, two hours from twilight, took the same path that I remembered taking as a boy in my pre-driver's license days.

There was a new subdivision in the first field that I always skirted on my way to the pond, but the tiny branch whose waters snaked

107

around a dilapidated woven wire fence in a clump of trees had not changed much that I could tell.

The ragged, smoky clouds that hung on the treetops had brought a mixture of snowflakes and light, freezing rain.

There was a familiar exhilaration about it -- the snow, the russet fields of faded autumn tints, trimmed with charcoal-colored tree lines.

I began looking for the circular stand of trees that guarded my secret place.

In front of me was an old bog, treeless and grown over with weeds. This could not be it.

There it was, in the distance. But again I was wrong. It was only a clump of trees.

I chuckled, imagining myself for a moment as a thirsty prospector racing from one mirage to the next.

Then, over the next rise, the pond suddenly came into view, just as it had nearly 30 years before.

I stood for a moment, just looking at it, and liking it, feeling the restfulness that always descended on me here.

Had 27 years really passed since I last stood here, wearing my four-buckle overshoes and with snowflakes in my eyelashes, reveling in the sight of a glorified mudhole?

No ducks were on the pond this time, and the spring-fed pool looked smaller than I remembered, but the sight of it was like a reunion with an old friend.

Less than an hour of daylight was left, and though a picture would not do the place justice, I raised the camera.

Later, I walked up for a close look at the spot that had so mysteriously embedded itself in my memory, and savored the treat of finding it virtually undisturbed, its charm and tranquility intact.

I studied it for a good while, hoping to remember the way it looked this day, as I had at dusk nearly three decades earlier. And I wondered if I was crazy, coming here on New Year's Eve in weather like this to visit a pond.

No, I was all right, I decided; it's just that I don't turn loose of yesterdays very easily.

Dusk and snowflakes enveloped my secret place as I took one last, distant look; then, reluctantly, I wandered off into another decade.

The 'Sleeping Prophet'

November 13, 1989

HOPKINSVILLE, Ky. -- Edgar Cayce was known by many names -- the sleeping prophet, miracle man, America's greatest mystic, and even the freak.

Cayce was born on a farm in southern Christian County on March 18, 1877. As a small boy he told his parents of having visions, of seeing and talking to dead relatives, of hearing a voice speak from a bright light that appeared to him.

His family, convinced at first that young Edgar had an overactive imagination fed by religious revivals that were then sweeping the region, largely ignored his claims.

Their son was not an especially good student and seemed uninterested in games other children enjoyed. He preferred to be alone, reading the Bible and meditating, and his formal education ended with the seventh grade.

As a young man he worked as a photographer, but he was to eventually become an internationally famous clairvoyant. He spoke while in self-induced hypnotic trances on such diverse subjects as medicine, science, world affairs, natural calamities and religion.

His many followers claimed that Cayce was able to diagnose illnesses, prescribe cures and foretell world events with amazing accuracy.

In 1934 Cayce predicted that during the latter portion of the 40 years before 1998, there would be widespread destruction in Los Angeles, San Francisco and New York. He visualized that the Great Lakes would one day empty into the Gulf of Mexico, that parts of Georgia, the Carolinas and Florida would be inundated, that portions of Japan would slide into the sea and that cataclysmic changes would occur in northern Europe.

He spoke of a striking reversal of global climates, and in 1943 he warned America: "The hardships for this country have not yet begun, so far as the demand for food is concerned. Anyone who can buy a farm is fortunate. And buy it, if you don't want to grow hungry in days to come."

Cayce historians say that he not only predicted the two world wars but also when they would begin and end, and that he forecast the Great Depression and the stock-market crash of 1929. Six months before the crash, he reportedly warned his friends to sell their stock.

A few months before his death in 1945, Cayce visualized the end of communism in Russia, and he predicted that a free Russia would eventually form a friendly alliance with the United States.

Despite his limited formal education, Cayce was reputed to have been well-versed on any subject he spontaneously discussed with questioners while "sleeping." He often astonished physicians with his knowledge of medicine and anatomy while in his trance. When awakened, he claimed to remember nothing of what he had said and to be unfamiliar with words he had spoken.

He rarely had much money, and he was convinced that using his psychic gift for his own financial gain was not only ethically wrong but harmful to his health.

He was a devout believer in reincarnation, confident that he had lived before and that he would return in another life. He admired Abraham Lincoln and Robert E. Lee, and he studied the Bible relentlessly.

God's Ad Man

November 16, 1983

MIDDLESBORO, Ky. -- If you've ever passed a large white concrete cross on a highway, bearing the inscription "Get Right With God," chances are it was made and placed there by Henry Harrison Mayes.

If you've wondered who's responsible for the corrugated metal signs in the shapes of hearts and crosses that say "Jesus Is Coming Soon," "Jesus Saves," and "Prepare to Meet God," Mayes erected most of those, too.

Even airports were not ignored by God's self-appointed advertising agent, who says that he managed to place large letters, visible from the air, within one mile of nearly 50 airport runways around the Southeast, warning those who might look out the airplane windows to "Prepare To Meet God."

From a two-page picture in Life magazine, to National Geographic, Newsweek and Grit, pictures of and stories about Mayes and his crosses and signs have, over the years, been a recurring symbol of religious fervor in Appalachia.

Now 85 and wearing his second pacemaker, Mayes struggles to recall when and how it all began.

"I guess I was 14 or 15 when I started organizing Sunday schools and having prayer meetings, and writing small signs on old rough brogan paper like they used to have tacked on telephone poles. Then I got to painting them on rocks, then on bigger things."

His signs, warning passers-by to repent, are now scattered across 44 states.

Mayes figures that he and his wife of 66 years, Lillie, have spent at least $75,000 of their own money making and delivering signs across the country, although he says that business people and churches around Middlesboro have been kind enough to help out when asked.

A good many years back he built a 140-foot-tall lighted cross that stands on a mountaintop overlooking Middlesboro.

"I finally got to where I couldn't pay the electric bill on it," he said, "but the lights still come on every night. I don't know who's paying the bill."

112

Most of Mayes' crosses and signs were made and placed during what little spare time he could find in the 43 years that he worked as a coal miner in Bell County.

"For several years after I got to putting signs on the highways I didn't know what a bed was," he said. "I'd get my signs ready in the winter and load them up and take them off in the spring and summer."

Many nights, while on the road in faraway states, he slept on the ground, under the truck, covered with a tarpaulin.

He has been cursed, run off and threatened with a gun, but none of it seems to have dampened his spiritual zeal.

"I like to have got robbed four or five times," Mayes said. "I just outwitted them, that's all."

Age and a heart condition, coupled with the effects of a mining accident and what he calls "old-time rheumatism," finally forced him to stop distributing concrete crosses and metal signs across the country in 1975. But his one-man crusade continues.

"You know, the Lord wants us to use horse sense," he commented. "Now, he puts all the berries out there, but he's not gonna come down here and pick 'em and give 'em to me. It's my job to get 'em."

Unable to travel as he once did, Mayes has turned to what might be called a "bottle ministry," which has its headquarters in a cluttered back room of his modest home on Chester Avenue in Middlesboro.

He buys empty, throw-away bottles that have been washed, places religious messages inside them, seals them with a cork and some glue, then sends them to missionaries and friends around the world, asking them to throw the bottles into streams, lakes and oceans.

"I just sent off 120 bottles to missionaries in the United States yesterday," Mayes said. "I go over here to Pineville sometimes and just throw out a bunch of 'em over there," in the Cumberland River.

"Well, they're headed for New Orleans. And when they get into the Gulf of Mexico, the Gulf stream ... the tides and hurricanes switches 'em everywhere."

Inside each bottle, where it may be read through the glass, is a piece of paper that says, "Prepare to meet God," printed not only in English, but in several foreign languages as well. Twenty of Mayes' personal proverbs, dealing with a wide range of moral and political issues, are also contained in the message. So far he has sent out 56,000 bottles, he says, all over the world. Each bottle is dated, and each carries Mayes' name and address.

Among the many letters he has received in response to his bottle ministry was one from a lumberjack in Washington state who found Mayes' message in a whiskey bottle on the bank of a stream, deep in the woods.

A resident of the island of Guam found one of the bottles on the beach, several years after it had been released.

Yes, he is aware of the laws against littering, Mayes said. But he is about the Lord's work, and he can't stop.

"All in the world I'm trying to do is help people," he said. "That's all."

The ABC's of Nature
April 16, 1990

A natural alphabet -- formed by the limbs and roots of trees -- is a jumbled epitaph to the late Rob Wilson, who spent 50 years searching the woods along the Kentucky-Tennessee border while gathering the unusual collection.

Wilson grew up in Taylor County, Ky., but spent much of his life in Pickett County, Tenn., which adjoins Clinton County, Ky. He died in Pickett County in 1973 at age 88.

He worked at a few odd jobs, but mostly he made and bottomed chairs.

What got him interested in collecting twigs and roots that resembled letters might remain a mystery forever, although it is presumed that during his frequent trips into the woods in search of white oak for chair bottoms, he often saw odd limb formations that might have inspired his collection.

Wilson was illiterate but had a gift for rhyme. He often dictated to his children or grandchildren long "poems" about people, places and things, which were written in longhand, and which he later published. There were 13 booklets of his work, and several still exist.

Many of his simple rhyming narratives are religious, but others cover such diverse subjects as vehicles, traders, politics, Gen. Douglas MacArthur and the evils of women's shorts.

Wilson was widely known in Pickett County and beyond, what with his books of verse, his natural alphabet and his chair-making skill.

Ruth Moles, 54, the librarian in Pickett County, remembers him as a good-natured fellow who roamed the countryside on foot and who was considered one of the colorful characters of Byrdstown, Tenn., in his later years.

A granddaughter of Wilson, Reba Byrd, 52, of Byrdstown, recalled that her grandfather was tall, always wore a hat and usually had on work clothes. He picked a banjo and loved to dance, she said.

And, Byrd said, "he would get out and go into the woods every day and hunt for those trees. He kind of kept the alphabet hidden."

Eventually, the alphabet was bought by the late Dr. Floyd Hay of Albany, Ky., who displayed it in his office for several years.

115

Wilson told Hay that he searched seven years before finding the letter "Q." His collection consists of at least one of every letter in the alphabet and duplicates of many, in various woods. It also contains the numbers through 9.

Hay died a few years ago, and his friend Dr. Steve Aaron, a Louisville surgeon with family ties to Adair County, eventually acquired the alphabet. Aaron now has the letters mounted on boards and displayed at his home.

He said Wilson -- presumably with help from others -- often had the letters arranged to form Bible verses, and on one large board that is still intact, he paid tribute to the late President John F. Kennedy.

Generally, the letters are not carved or whittled, although a few have been trimmed in a place or two.

"Apparently, he carried them around with him and decided he was sort of a missionary," Aaron said. "You can marvel at the gumption it took for him to gather all of these.

"It's art, because it's the end product of some individual's creativity. Even though Rob was illiterate, letters were very important to him. You can look at them and see that a letter, to him, was just like a silver dollar."

Kentucky Characters I

February 24, 1988

Does anyone remember "The Goat Man"?

That's what we called him in south-central Kentucky when I was a boy. The Goat Man.

Once every four or five years, word would spread that the Goat Man had passed through the quiet farming community where I lived. I wonder now whether I really saw him once, or whether I just dreamed it. In my memory, he was a stocky, stoop-shouldered fellow with a white beard who plodded along beside the highway, with 15 or 20 or more goats scattered about him.

We always thought he was just a nomad who wandered all over the country with his goats.

There weren't very many goats in our neck of the woods back then, and if farmers ever saw a stray goat, they automatically deduced that the Goat Man must have passed through.

Some folks may have laughed at the Goat Man, but with me he was accorded legendary status, almost equal to that of Santa Claus, Red Ryder, Johnny Philip Morris and Mark Trail (a comic-strip character).

I probably wouldn't have thought about the Goat Man had a friend not mentioned to me the other day that the quantity and quality of colorful characters appears to have declined in these parts in recent years.

He was right.

The likes of Walking Ben Wilson of Anderson County, who walked barefoot to the Kentucky State Fair every year, or Silas Sullivan of Russell County, a perennial, unsuccessful candidate for public office with a gift for oratory, are rarely found these days.

These men may have been eccentric, but they were witty and philosophical, and nice to have around when life got monotonous.

I have heard that there was a fellow in Edmonson County years ago who was called "The Rat Man." I suppose he was a rat exterminator.

Then there was "Walking Mun Wilson," from Hopkins County, who hung around Frankfort a lot, and walked every place he went.

117

Former Gov. A.B. "Happy" Chandler remembers that Walking Mun had been elected to a term in the Kentucky House, probably back in the 1920s.

"He didn't look like he had any great intellect... and I don't think he did," Chandler said. "He looked like he had been sent for and couldn't go. He was a small fellow...with long hair, and he just lived by what he got from folks around. The first time I was governor, he came to my house for breakfast nearly every morning.

"The cook had orders to take care of him, and she'd ask him what he wanted. He'd say, 'Just give me whatever you gave the governor.'"

Mun prided himself on walking all over Kentucky and would generally refuse a ride if it was offered, Chandler said.

If you have stories about such characters that you'd like to share with our readers, send them along to me.

And while you're at it, would someone be kind enough to tell me where the Goat Man came from, and what happened to him?

The Goat Man

March 4, 1988

The Goat Man lives!

My recent column about colorful characters of Kentucky's bygone days, including my vague recollections of having seen a fellow called "the Goat Man," brought immediate response from many readers.

So far, about 50 of you have written or called to confirm that there really was  a Goat Man who traveled around the country and sometimes passed through Kentucky with a bunch of goats pulling a rickety wagon.

Several of you sent copies of a recent column by Joe Dorris in the Hopkinsville New Era, in which Dorris quotes a recent full-page newspaper story from Macon, Ga., (sent to him by one of his readers) that said the Goat Man -- Charles "Chess" McCartney -- is living at the Eastview Nursing Home in Macon, where he was taken after losing two toes to frostbite in February, 1987.

The story notes that McCartney's reign as the Goat Man began about the time of the Great Depression, when he lost his farm in his native Iowa. Although he often returned to Iowa in the summer, he made his home -- when not on the road with his goats --on a small tract of land he owned at Jeffersonville, near Macon.

Randall Savage, who interviewed McCartney for the Macon Telegraph and News, told me that the Goat Man -- who says he's 103 but whose medical records indicate him to be 87 -- is still alert, talkative and "very road wise." He adds that the Goat Man has struck up a heavy courtship with one of the women at the nursing home, who keeps insisting that the two are married.

The "goat cavalcade," as he sometimes called it, was disbanded in 1969, and the Goat Man says he gave his goats to Walt Disney World.

Those of you who wrote and called had many wonderful memories of the Goat Man which, collectively, paint a nice profile of this unusual character.

Evidently he sold or gave away lots of postcards with his pictures on them over the years, and readers have sent me seven or eight different Goat Man postcards, both in color and black and white.

Sue Harrison of Louisville wrote, "I am sending you this picture of him with his young son, Gene, and his wife. He did not have his wife with him as he passed through Clinton County, but he always had his son."

Sue, I understand that the son still resides on the land where he lived with his father near Macon.

Lisa Harbolt of Louisville says her family has a five-minute, 1950s-vintage home movie film clip of the Goat Man.

Vicki Nordmann of Louisville, whose father took her out Bardstown Road near Buechel to see the Goat Man sometime in the early to mid-1950s, writes, "As best I can remember, he had a long, white beard and carried a staff or walking stick, but I may have this confused with Heidi's grandfather."

Although most postcards show him with a dark beard, he did have a white beard nearly down to his waist at one time, Vicki. I'm told he now has a short beard.

Ruth Ann Street of Louisville, who saw the Goat Man near Hopkinsville when she was a child, recalls that he was a "medium-sized, hairy man, whose bare feet where like leather. He wore overalls...with no shirt and one strap connected over his shoulder. He would come down Highway 41, heading south, in late fall every year."

Twice, between 1936 and '39, Kay Shephard of Louisville saw him come through Albany, in Clinton County, with about 20 goats.

Dennie Davidson of Burkesville recalls that a team of mules, pulling a wagon, once spooked and ran off with his father and a neighbor when they met the Goat Man on the road in Cumberland County.

Allen Grider of Glasgow says that the Goat Man came through Russell County about 1950 or '51; that his "lead goat" at the time was named "Woosie"; and that "the whole lot stunk worse than a gut wagon."

Pearl Yates of Louisville found a clipping from the Oct. 5, 1953, Courier-Journal about the Goat Man's visit to the Buechel area. At that time, his caravan consisted of 27 goats, some wearing bells, and an ancient, steel-wheeled wagon covered with lanterns, license plates, hubcaps, mirrors, bottles, an unoccupied bird house and other odds and ends.

His wife had left him, and he sat in an aluminum chair that had been an airplane seat, gulping coffee from a quart jar, the article said.

Jodie Hall of Leitchfield, a columnist for the Grayson County News-Gazette, says the Goat Man once told him in Georgia that when he came to a hill, the goats following the wagon would push.

It's true, says Bill Mack of Shelbyville, who years ago followed the Goat Man for a considerable distance through the hills of East Tennessee. The goats that ambled along behind the wagon would push -- on command -- when extra power was needed.

Long live the Goat Man!

Kentucky Characters II

March 9, 1988

Our reader search for colorful characters out of Kentucky's past has yielded a number of interesting subjects in addition to the Goat Man, who was covered in a previous column.

"Russell County had an unusual character by the name of Asa Scholl . . . a bachelor, who boarded at several homes about the county," writes Allen Grider of Glasgow. "After leaving one of the places of abode, he met his former landlady on the street in Jamestown. She angrily confronted him by saying, 'Asa Scholl, people are telling me that you had to leave my house because the cooking was so nasty you could no longer eat it.'

"Mr. Asa gave a respectful bow and said, 'Lady, I don't know who told you that, but they spoke God's truth.'

"She was so dumbfounded by such honesty that she replied, 'Don't you know that you have to eat a certain amount of nastiness before you die?'

" 'Yes, ma'am,' Asa politely replied, 'but I don't want to eat it all at once.' "

My old friend and mentor, Ralph Cress of Danville, remembers a host of colorful characters who lived in, or traveled through, Kentucky.

Twice, Cress says, he saw a man who came out of Missouri driving a covered wagon with a three-mule hitch, with a couple of "spare mules" tied to the back. He had a couple of dogs and a small flock of bantam chickens.

"When the wagon stopped, the chickens would get off and start pecking around; then, when he got ready to move, he'd call them and they would load back up," Cress said. "While he was moving, the rooster would ride atop the hames of the lead mule. Quite a sight."

Cress also remembers four or five wagonloads of Gypsies that came through every August, camped at the corner of his family's farm, and spent two or three days trying to trade horses with local farmers.

"While they were there, Mom counted her chickens every morning."

Cress remembers Buster Brown and his dog, Tige, who visited stores that stocked Buster Brown Shoes. Buster, dressed in a red suit and sailor hat, gave children little tin crickets to snap.

"Local legends -- How about Lee Chrisman, who stood on top of the Gilcher Hotel in Danville and yelled 'Ya-hoo!' and was heard eight miles away?

"Don't forget the old umbrella repairman, the pot and pan fixers, and the knife and scissors sharpeners who traveled throughout the country, going from house to house...and the organ grinders and their monkeys," Cress said.

"When I was a kid, back in the '20s and early '30s, there was a world of stuff going though the country to see -- cows with 7-foot horns, 1,200-pound hogs...a little guy who let them bust rocks on his chest, and let a gasoline truck run over him. And they only cost you 10 cents.

"You would have really had a ball back in those days. It's just a crying shame things got better before you came along."

Edgar Arnold of Madisonville says that "Walking Mun Wilson," mentioned in an earlier column, was Munnell Wilson, who served at least one term in the legislature from Hopkins County.

"He was noted for walking everywhere, even to Frankfort and back, but he didn't always turn down a ride," Arnold said. "The late 'Abe' Moore, a noted attorney here, often told of giving Munn a ride to Frankfort, picking him up along the road not far from Madisonville. When they were almost to the Capitol City, Munn asked to get out, saying, 'I can't be seen riding with a lawyer for the big coal companies.' "

"Munn made lots of speeches underneath the 'tree of knowledge' on the courthouse yard here, and also preached some."

Finally, John M. Russell of Cox Creek, Ky., writes: "During the Depression year of 1930, there was an old man who lived in a huge hollow tree in the woods at the north end of Virginia Avenue and

Harris Place, near the L & N Railroad (in the Lyndon area of eastern Jefferson County).

"The old gent earned the name 'Coffee,' as he would make his rounds to numerous homes in the area, always approaching the back door with a request, ' Please, ma'am, can you spare a cup of coffee?'

"Most always his request was granted, along with a leftover biscuit or piece of pie."

One day a friend of Russell's had been hunting and was cleaning his shotgun when Coffee knocked at the back door.

Not thinking, the friend carried his gun to the door, and when Coffee saw it, he ran for his life and was not seen again.

Thank you all for your "character" references.

Hog Wild

September 13, 1989

Among the ivy thickets and rock cliffs of a few counties in southeastern Kentucky lives a seldom seen animal that the Kentucky Department of Fish and Wildlife hopes will one day be extinct in the state -- the wild hog.

Its presence has been confirmed in Estill, Lee, McCreary, Wayne and Whitley counties.

A few wild hogs had been reported in Marion County, but Richard Hines, wildlife biologist for the south-central district, says there have been no such reports there since the animal was placed on the state's varmint list between 1985 and 1987.

Hines theorizes that some of the wild hogs of European (perhaps Russian) stock that now inhabit the hills of McCreary, Wayne and Whitley counties, and neighboring counties in Tennessee, descended from animals that were brought to a shooting preserve that once operated in the area.

When the preserve closed, the European wild hogs eventually were turned loose or escaped and interbred with free-roaming feral hogs of domestic species.

The product of this cross is generally grayish in color, with a long snout. It also is smaller, with slimmer hindquarters but more powerful shoulders, than domestic animals.

The young, up to the age of about 3 months, have light stripes on their backs. Although it is illegal to import wild hogs into Kentucky, or to possess them, there exists a kind of backwoods black market on the animals through which illegal "midnight stockings" often occur.

That is how Hines believes wild hogs came to be in Lee, Estill and Marion counties.

A few years ago some wild hogs were confiscated and destroyed in Breathitt County and, at one time, even Boone County in Northern Kentucky had a small population.

Those who have hunted Kentucky's wild hogs have found them far more elusive than most other larger wildlife species.

They are secretive, not usually aggressive unless threatened, tend to stay in small groups, and feed on acorns and nearly any other kind of available plant or animal life.

It is the wild hog's indiscriminate foraging habits that make it a particularly undesirable species, game biologists say. In addition to destroying most forms of plant life in areas in which it roots for food, biologists note that the wild hog will feed on the nests and young of all ground nesting birds, such as grouse, quail and turkey, and on the young of many other animals.

The animal also may carry swine brucellosis, cholera, pseudorabies and other diseases transmissible to domestic hogs.

The wild hog was removed from the year-round varmint list after a few sportsmen's groups became concerned that some hunters were using the hog season to hunt for deer out of season.

Wild hogs may now be taken only during deer season -- with either a gun or bow by legal deer hunters. But last deer season only one hog was reported killed -- in McCreary County.

Hines says the wild hog population in Lee County seems to be increasing fairly rapidly. He has been told that it is also on the rise in Scott and Pickett counties in Tennessee, while numbers appear to be increasing only slightly in McCreary. No estimate was available from Estill County.

"It's like managing a ghost," Hines said of efforts to monitor the wild hog. "Every once in a while you'll get a glimpse of one. But most of the time, all you're looking at is signs . . . and there's no rhyme or reason to their foraging habits. Three may leave as much sign as 20, and 20 may leave as much sign as three."

Although the wild hog problem is not serious yet, Hines says the biological potential for problems is of concern.

"The population could appear to be rather stagnant for 10 or 11 years, then in a matter of eight to 10 months, things could just double or triple," he said.

Out of Pocket

January 10, 1990

DANVILLE, Ky. -- A wallet stolen in 1945 has finally found its way home.

Virginia Broyles said she was working as a cashier at a drugstore in Danville in December 1945 when someone lifted the wallet out of her purse.

Her husband, W.G. Broyles, was in the Navy at the time and had sent her the leather wallet, embossed with the Navy insignia.

At the time the wallet was stolen, Virginia Broyles ran an ad in the Danville paper hoping to recover it, but it never turned up, until late last week -- 44 years later.

That's when a passerby spotted the wallet lying in the street that crosses a viaduct on the western edge of town and turned it in at the Danville Police headquarters.

"Detective Ed Alsman called from the police station last Friday and said he thought he had something that belonged to me," Virginia Broyles explained. "Well, I had no idea. I said, 'I don't know of anything that's gone.'

"He came out here and handed me that billfold, and I looked at it, and it came open, and I said, 'Well there's our picture.' I had even forgotten what the billfold looked like. I got to looking, and I said, 'Why that was lost in 1945.' He looked at me...and didn't know what to say."

Alsman said he at first assumed the wallet had been discarded by a burglar who had recently taken it from someone's home.

"It kind of stunned me when she said it was something that had occurred 45 years ago," Alsman said.

He now suspects that the wallet was either left on the street by someone in Danville who had stolen it those many years ago and had a guilty conscience, or perhaps by someone passing through town during the holidays who had lived in Danville when the wallet was stolen and decided to unburden himself or herself of it while passing through.

Some gas- and sugar-ration stamps and a small amount of money (Virginia Broyles doesn't remember exactly how much) were missing from the wallet, but its other contest -- her 1945 driver's license, a Social Security card and several photos -- were still inside and in good condition.

There is a picture of the Broyleses that was taken in 1943, when both were in their 30s. He is now 80 and she is 76.

The other pictures are of W.G. in his Navy uniform, except for one in which he is wearing a suit, tie and white shoes, standing beside a 1937 Ford.

Broyles, a retired auto mechanic, said he vaguely remembers sending his wife the wallet from one of his duty stations in the Navy, but he doesn't remember where he bought it, and he didn't recognize it when police returned it last week.

"I had fussed more about losing the pictures than anything," Virginia Broyles recalled.

Now she not only has her pictures back, but an interesting conversation piece, as well -- "if somebody doesn't come along and get it again."

Up, Up and a Spray

September 1, 1991

BLOOMFIELD, Ky. -- "I've been around this territory so long that I consider a lot of people as friends that I don't even know," Tommy Howard said. "I'll fly over, and they'll wave, and I'll wiggle the wings at them, or throw my hand out."

Howard, 57, long ago lost count of how many thousands of hours he has flown as an agricultural spray pilot, but he has kept track of the number of years -- 35.

That's how long he has been hopping fence rows, ducking power lines and skimming treetops in the old Piper Cub he flies, then racing darkness back to a landing strip on the farm where he and his wife, Jo Ann, live near Bloomfield.

When Howard took over his father's crop-dusting business at age 22, he had already been flying five or six years. In those days, crop dusters were known for their daredevil antics, and Howard admits to his share.

"I used to like to see just how close to something I could get without hitting it, and I've hit a few things -- trees, wires and barns," he said. "I left two wheel marks on a barn roof one time, but that was unintentional."

Once a wire caught a wing and flipped the plane toward the ground, Howard said, but the left wheel bounced off the ground, "and I got back in the air and kept flying, and came home."

"Dad was sitting out there, and I taxied in with the wing all torn up.

"He said, 'My goodness, Tommy, it's going to take three days to fix that airplane.'

"I said, 'It's going to take two to clean it out.' "

Through most of the spring and summer, Howard is often busy from daylight to dark spraying for insects and weeds on farms within a radius of about 50 miles of Bardstown.

Jo Ann -- his high school sweetheart, wife of 38 years and the mother of the couple's two sons -- handles everything but the flying, Howard said. She not only keeps books, but also checks out the plane and refuels before each flight.

"I hate airplanes," she said, "and you worry. You never quit worrying. But he enjoys it so well that I do what I can to make it easier for him. He always wanted me to learn to fly, but I said, 'I'm not going to do it. If I learn to fly, he'll make me spray.' "

More than once she has waited at the end of the airfield with the trucks's headlights aimed at the landing strip so Howard could see to bring the plane in from a late run or on nights when fog settled in unexpectedly. On one such occasion she remembers pulling down the radio antenna on top of the truck so he wouldn't hit it as he passed overhead.

In his 35 years of crop spraying, Howard has seen enough to fill several books.

"Some things are unspeakable. You never mention them," he said. "You'll see so-and-so with so-and-so's wife out here someplace, you know, but you don't see it either.

'I've been accused of circling houses to watch women sunbathing, when I was working, and didn't even see them," he said. "But it's not above me to make an extra turn."

Then there was the woman, unfamiliar with Howard's Spray Service, who phoned the Bardstown airport one day and reported sighting a red-and-white plane that was "trying to crash."

Law-enforcement authorities sometimes seek his help in finding missing persons.

There have been many close calls. Once the plane was caught in a large whirlwind and Howard lost control for a few seconds before getting the aircraft back on course.

A slug from a high-caliber rifle hit the plane once, but the man who fired it claimed it was an accident, and there was no serious damage.

Another time the plane ran out of gas in a turn and stopped running, but Howard was able to switch to his reserve tank and restart the engine just before the aircraft reached the ground.

Several times he has discovered that he was within inches of wires that he did not know were there, and sometimes he hears them rub the plane when he doesn't know where they are.

Howard said he'd like to quit crop spraying when he is 60, because he thinks that reflexes and eyesight diminish significantly at that age, and he doesn't want to push his luck.

For now, he and the 1953 model Piper Super Cub that he has flown for years are still hopping fence rows and skimming treetops.

"I bought a new Piper Super Cub in 1979...but I don't like to fly it," Howard said. "In the old one, it seems like I can pull up to the end of the field and just think left and it'll turn left. The other one's controls are stiff and I have to fly it every inch of the way.

"Or maybe I just don't want to tear up the good one."

Speedy Stalker
August 8, 1990

LANCASTER, Ky. -- "He's just a tobacco-cutting machine. As a matter of fact, he's better than the machines I've seen."

That's how Garrard County's agricultural extension agent, Mike Carter, describes tobacco cutter Bobby Preston, who Tuesday afternoon cut 216 sticks of burley tobacco in 47 minutes and 2 seconds to claim $300 in prize money and a handsome trophy declaring him "World Champion."

It is the ninth straight year that Preston, a 35-year-old father of two, Garrard County Water Co. employee and part-time farmer, has won the contest.

"When he cuts for other people, *he* cuts the tobacco and there is a crew that follows him," Carter said. "It's amazing. He's fluid motion."

Preston, who is 6-feet-4 and weighs 190, says he started cutting tobacco at about age 8 as a farm boy in Garrard County.

"I think it's something you grow up with," he said. "My father was a fast cutter, and everybody he cut against was fast, so I've been racing since I was a kid."

Although he has a few secrets that he thinks may give him a racing edge, Preston modestly attributes most of his speed to long arms and long legs, concentration, natural rhythm and common sense.

"I never do stand up and look around to see what everybody else is doing. You can't do that," he said.

For those unfamiliar with tobacco cutting, smooth sticks about 4 feet long are dropped end-to-end between two rows of tobacco. Cutters advance, alternating rows as they cut, jamming one end of each stick into the dirt. Then they slide each stalk of burley onto the stick over a metal spear on the end of the stick. When six stalks have been speared on a stick, the process is repeated.

At top speed, Preston averages cutting and spearing a stalk about every two seconds.

"Three hundred and two is the most sticks I've ever cut in one hour, and I think it's the most I *can* cut," Preston said. "I have cut 1,500 sticks in seven hours. I've seen plenty of cutters that could stay with me all day, but nobody's ever beaten me in one hour."

Cutters are judged not only on speed but efficiency, and are penalized for sticks that fall over and stalks that split out. Two years ago another Garrard Countian, James Gilbert Edgington, beat Preston to the end of the row by a few seconds, but lost in overall scoring when the split-out stalks and overturned sticks were counted. Edgington finished third yesterday behind Preston's cousin, Kevin Preston, among six contestants.

Originally, the contest, which sometimes draws more than 600 spectators to various farms on which it is held, was called the Garrard County Tobacco Cutting Contest. Last year its name was changed to the World Champion Tobacco Cutting Contest.

"Other counties that have tried to have contests won't let our boys come in," Mike Carter said.

"Our contest is open to anybody from anywhere. I'm not saying it can't happen, but Bobby Preston will have to be beaten by somebody to convince me that he's not the world champion."

Preston's 5-year-old tobacco knife, or tomahawk, and his spear are standard models that he bought at a local farm-supply store. It helps, he says, to practice a little each year before the contest.

His job as a serviceman for the local water company gives him plenty of exercise, but Preston is a pack-and-a-half-a-day smoker, and he has no special conditioning program to stay in shape for the contest.

"I never do eat the hamburgers that they serve right before the contest," Preston said. "I usually wait until after it's over."

A Face in the Cloud

July 12, 1993

Have you ever raced with a cloud?

On sultry summer days like these -- in a time that seems an eternity ago, yet is really only a sweet yesterday -- I once scampered barefoot across a big field in a footrace with the sky.

Cloud shadows swept across the flat field behind our farmhouse like the surf on Cape Fear; narrow, dark bands, moving swiftly, sometimes slowly, on bright, fluffy days when I guessed the whole world was asleep except the clouds and me.

God himself lived in the clouds, or at least had the use of them when He wanted. I saw Him peering at me sometimes from gleaming isles suspended somewhere beyond the creek at the back of our place. He had a majestic, fleecy beard, all-seeing eyes that often shone as blue as the sky itself, and hair that swirled into the heavens like the figures on the ceiling of the Sistine Chapel. But Michelangelo had neither time nor enough oil to paint, in a lifetime, what I saw in the clouds on lazy summer days.

Sometimes I saw angels -- wings and all -- or the devil, or old seamen, ships and whales, giant birds and great herds of buffalo. And occasionally, a clown with a marshmallow face would be there looking at me, but would melt away as I was calling someone to see, and only a misshapen nose or one eye would remain when I returned with a witness.

Not every day was a good cloud-racing day, only the ones on breezy summer days, when the clouds floated like mounds of whipped cream in the blue yonder. Then I would notice the cloud shadows skimming the locust treetops on a distant knoll, and would know that soon they would pass over me, and sail on toward Tennessee.

It took awhile to get onto it -- racing with clouds. There is, after all, no fair start with a cloud. You have to be running when the race begins, as relay runners or trotting horses do. By starting to run when the cloud shadow was 30 or 40 feet behind me, then keeping my eyes on the ground until the shadow drew even, I figured to give the cloud a good race until we came to a fence or one of us ran out of wind.

I do not remember how many races I won. The win was less important to me than the bigness of it all. Racing with things that God lived in, that airplanes flew through, that lightning came from. Maybe I was only running on the edge of a shadow, but I was, in those few frantic, glorious seconds, able to look down and see my own two grimy little feet chasing the sky across the Earth.

A cloud shadow, the first I had noticed in a long time, washed over me last week on the edge of a bluegrass meadow, and it set me to wondering. Do kids today still see faces in the clouds? Do they ever look at the sky? Do they know about racing with clouds?

Back at home, hours later, I asked my 16-year-old son if he had ever heard of such a thing.

"Do you mean with the shadows that come over?"

"You know about it," I said with satisfaction. "Have you ever done it?"

"I think I have," he said, "on the tennis court."

Bluegrass Savannas

January 16, 1991

Some of the strangest and most interesting natural wonders of Kentucky's Bluegrass region are the picturesque remnants of the Bluegrass savannas that still exist on numerous farms in Central Kentucky.

Loosely defined, a savanna is a tract of level land covered, in part, with low vegetation and few trees.

"The Bluegrass savanna has a lot more tree cover than the savannas in Africa or the Caribbean, but that's what they're called in the Bluegrass, for better or worse," said Tom Bloom, a botanist with the Kentucky Nature Preserves Commission.

When the first white settlers arrived in what is now Central Kentucky, they found vast expanses of land covered with prairie grasses and small bushes, and scattered with large trees.

Years later, researchers would puzzle over the "Bluegrass savannas"-- or "savanna woodlands," as Thomas More College biologist Bill Bryant called them in a study conducted several years ago.

"I use the word 'woodland' because the trees were dominant, although widely spaced," Bryant said. "The dominant trees (200 years ago) would have been basically the same kind that are there today: burr oak, blue ash, chinquapin oak, shumard oak, shagbark and shellbark hickory. The ground cover is what has really changed. Probably you would have had some wild rye and buffalo clover."

Naturalists say that at some point in the past a major disturbance must have opened large areas of the Kentucky forest, enabling nature to form the savannas.

"There are lots of things it could have been," Bloom said. "Approximately eight to 10 thousand years ago there was a glacial period, when glaciers reached down into southern Ohio.

"After it warmed back up again, there was a warm, dry period that occurred throughout this part of the world, maybe for a few thousand years, that probably caused a lot of this area to turn into prairie-like vegetation and produced a climate much like that of the Great Plains."

The changes in climate, coupled with heavy grazing by giant herds of bison and elk, and, later, the burning of some hunting grounds by Indians, as well as lightning fires, are all thought to have been factors that contributed to the savannas of the Bluegrass.

"To some extent they are artifacts," commented botanist Julian Campbell of the Nature Conservancy. "There is really nothing else quite like them in the world, especially in terms of the abundance of blue ash."

Most of the tree varieties found today in the savanna remnants of the Bluegrass are somewhat tolerant of fire, and many of the trees still there were already old when Kentucky was settled.

"I suspect that the city of Lexington is where it is because there was a large savanna there," Bloom said. "It was not as much work to clear a savanna as it was to clear a forest."

The study conducted by Bryant and other researchers indicated that a majority of the trees still living in Kentucky's savanna remnants were well over 300 years old, and that some of them were nearly 500. Several are lost each year to age, wind and lightning, or to development, and the savannas are gradually disappearing.

Stump of Contention

April 23, 1990

STEARNS, Ky. -- There is a 300-million-year-old story behind the sandstone tree stump that sits in the front yard of McCreary County's Stearns Museum.

Last summer a surface-mining company working in Tennessee near the Kentucky line unearthed the two-ton stump buried about 30 feet underground. It measures slightly more than 15 feet in circumference and almost six feet in diameter.

Several more feet of the fossilized trunk were broken apart at the mining site and could not be saved.

Billy J. Kidd of McCreary County, an employee of the mining company, loaded the stump onto his truck and brought it to the Stearns Museum, where a crane was used to place the unusual specimen in the yard.

"We have talked to people at the University of Kentucky, and they say it's not a petrified stump but a sandstone replacement of a tree that was growing 300 million to 315 million years ago," said Dr. Frank Thomas, retired former president of  the Stearns Coal and Lumber Co. and now a volunteer worker at the museum.

"I'd guess it was a large oak, but we're not sure," he said.

The tree had rotted out or dissolved and was replaced with sandstone rather than the petrified agate-like material found in the Petrified Forest, Thomas said.

Last year, not long after the stump was placed in front of the museum, former Tennessee Sen. Howard Baker stopped by for a visit and wondered aloud why -- since the stump was found in his native Scott County, Tenn. -- it wasn't on display there.

"Because you stole the land from us," Thomas told Baker.

Thomas says records show that when the southern boundary of Kentucky was being surveyed, the surveyor got turned around in the mountains and, as a result, the Kentucky state line is seven or eight miles too far north in some places.

"You can look at the Kentucky map, and when you get down to the Tennessee River (near Kentucky Lake), where it goes down and has that little notch in it, that notch shouldn't be there," Thomas said. The boundary line should run straight east all the way from the river to Virginia, he said.

If that is the case, the prehistoric sandstone stump would not merely be a wonder of nature but also a fitting monument to a magnificent blunder, too colossal to ever correct.

But at least Kentucky got the stump.

During the winter, Stearns Museum officials feared that if water got into cracks in the stump and froze, the artifact might crumble. So they covered it with a tarpaulin.

"We believe it needs to have a urethane coating of some kind on it to prevent the elements from getting in there," Thomas said. "We have to do that this summer because it is too nice an object to let it crumble."

So there the 300-million-year-old stone stump sits, for all who pass through the yard of the Stearns Museum to stop and admire, and for Kentuckians and Tennesseans to argue over for the next 300 million years.

The Siamese Car

September 15, 1991

CULVERTOWN, Ky. -- People usually do a double take -- and sometimes a triple -- when R. C. and Iona Bryan pass by in their 1954 Chevrolet. That's because it is not always easy to tell whether the Bryans are coming or going.

Their car, you see, looks the same on both ends, and even in the middle. It has two hoods, four headlights, two identical grilles, dashboards, gear shifts, radios, glove compartments and steering wheels, and two rear-view mirrors that face opposite directions.

"I've always wanted to try something different. You'd just have to ride with me sometime to see people's faces," Bryan said.
"We've had people meet us on the road and turn around and follow us home so they could see it," Iona added.

Most of the car's equipment is original, a combination of two '54 Chevys that Bryan artfully welded together a few years ago, just for the fun of it.

Bryan, 62, who once drove race cars on dirt tracks and retired after working 28 years as a carpenter at Fort Knox, said he had a few old cars that he had accumulated over the years, and he didn't know what to do with them.

"I had three '54 Chevys, and two of them were runable," he said. "They were all rusted down, and it would have cost too much to restore them.

"Every time I'd walk by them, I'd look at them and think, 'Something ought to be done with these.' Then's when I got to wondering if I could put two together and make something. I'd take my ruler with me and measure this and measure that, until finally, after about two months, I figured out how I could get two cars together."

Bryan went to work with his cutting torch in January 1988, and a few months later, out rolled a baby-blue and white '54 Chevy with two front ends.

One of the Chevys was a Bel-Air and the other was a Custom, but by the time Bryan finished with them, even he had trouble telling which end of the car was which.

"I got in that rascal one day and hit the key and nothing happened, and I figured maybe the battery cables were loose, so I got out, walked around to what I thought was the front -- and about that time it dawned on me what I had done, and I just sat back down in the car and laughed for about five minutes," Bryan recalled.

Only one end of the car has an engine in it -- the original 235-cubic-inch six-cylinder. Under one of the hoods there is only trunk space behind a dummy radiator.

The doors were cut in two, and handles were placed on each side of each door, although the doors are both hinged on the same side.

"He tells it as a joke that he doesn't know whether his mind is coming or going, so he built the car to match his mind. But I'm not so sure it's a joke," Iona said of her husband.

Since 1989, when the car made its debut on the parade circuit, the Bryans' phone has rung often with invitations to bring the car to parades.

They usually accept, if the parades are not too far away from Nelson County, and often they drive the car to such events -- Bryan facing one way behind the wheel, and his wife the other.

Friends said he could never build a second car that looked as good, so Bryan is building another -- this one matching the front half of a 1953 Pontiac with the front half of a '53 Chevy.

But wait, there's more.

"If nothing happens, I'm going to say that in three years from now, I'll have a car that you can fire up and drive from either end," he said. "You could go any way you wanted to; you could drive it in a parade sideways."

Sitting Cow
February 18, 1991

BURGIN, Ky. -- Everyone has heard of Sitting Bull, but only a handful of folks in Central Kentucky can tell you stories about Sitting Cow.

There was no rhyme or reason for her sitting, the late Worth Ensminger told me on my first visit to his Mercer County farm some years back. Sometimes he and his wife, Anne, would look out in the pasture and there she would sit, on her hindquarters, just as dogs and some other small four-legged animals do when they are resting.

"All the neighbors saw her first," Anne Ensminger recalled, "because she was out in the front field where we couldn't see."

Where did the cow ever get the idea to sit that way in the first place? Had she been watching the Ensmingers' dog, Phideaux, sitting across the fence watching the cows when suddenly it struck her to try it herself?

Apparently, others in the herd either could not master Sitting Cow's technique or thought the position inappropriate for a cow. Perhaps some of them tried it when no one was watching and embarrassed themselves so badly that they never tried again.

Sitting Cow, like the rest of the Ensmingers' herd, was a polled Hereford, a breed not generally known to have much personality and certainly not given to doing tricks.

Although the Ensmingers and the late John Woods, who was their farm manager, saw the cow sitting on numerous occasions and tried to photograph her several times, something always seemed to happen. They wouldn't have the camera loaded, or she would be out of camera range, or she would move before they could get ready. Worth Ensminger finally managed one slightly out-of-focus picture, which he had enlarged and framed.

Several reporters and photographers, myself included, tried to sneak up on the cow for a picture, but she would always graze contentedly until we left. Then, I suppose, she would find a place to sit and rest, and laugh.

Passing motorists sometimes stopped on the highway in front of the Ensminger farm to marvel at the cow, sitting alone in the pasture, as the rest of the herd stood or lay nearby, no doubt whispering among themselves about how different she was.

Occasionally, her sitting got in the way of her motherly duties. Ensminger complained that her calves would sometimes have to get down on their knees to nurse.

As the years clicked by, I kept thinking that, one day, blind luck would take me past the Ensminger place just as Sitting Cow sat. But it never happened.

The cow was finally sent to market a few years ago, and Worth Ensminger died in 1989.

His wife still has the color photograph of Sitting Cow, whose legend lives on around the stoves in feed stores and other places where farmers loaf in Mercer County during the winter.

No one is sure what happened to Sitting Cow's several offspring, but somewhere today I'll bet there are a few young polled Herefords sitting alone in pastures, wondering why they are different from other cows.

A Turtle Twosome

July 12, 1991

Todd Bitzer sure knows how to liven up a pool party. He just takes along his pet snapping turtle, 35-pound Samantha.

"I always know when there's a dirty swimming pool, because she wants to get in it," Bitzer said. "If there's chlorine in it, she'll stick her head down to the water and pull it back when she smells the chlorine."

Bitzer got the turtle 20 years ago, when he was 7 years old and Samantha was no bigger than a quarter. His older brother found her near their home in Anchorage in Jefferson County.

Samantha hibernates from November through most of March in a small tank in Bitzer's basement. The rest of the year her home is outdoors in a large, galvanized water tank where she usually stays submerged and comes out only long enough to eat fish, chicken and an occasional snack of dry dog food.

"She really has two personalities. She'll attack anything when she's in the tank, because she thinks it's food," Bitzer explained. "But when she's out, I've never had any trouble with her."

The turtle likes having her head, neck and legs rubbed, and doesn't mind being petted by strangers, as long as they don't pick her up by her tail.

"Sometimes when I'm driving down the road, she'll get under my arm and start nudging me, wanting to get in my lap," Bitzer said. "She really likes to be held, and when she's in your lap sometimes she just gets like a rag doll. You can pull her arms and legs and do anything with her."

Samantha's veterinarian, Dr. Jack Nightengale, believes that if she stays healthy, she could live to the age of 140, and Bitzer's friends are already urging him to provide for Samantha in his will. But for now, he and the turtle are having the time of their lives.

"It was just last year, really, that I started taking her out to different places," said Bitzer, 27, who is single and a construction worker.

A local saddle shop made a harness and leash for Samantha, and Bitzer and his turtle, besides going to pool parties, have gone out to eat at restaurants where there is outdoor dining.

Once they startled some ducks on a pond near one of the restaurants. At another establishment, Bitzer was told that Samantha could not stay with him as he ate at a table outdoors.

"I told them I didn't see why," Bitzer complained. "There were people with Doberman Pinschers there. But they said Samantha couldn't stay, so we left."

The turtle has been welcome most places he has taken her, Bitzer said, and even most of the women he has met have liked the turtle.

"I took her on a date one time to get rid of a girl," Bitzer recalled. "This girl nagged and was terrible, and I thought, 'How can I be nice and get rid of her?' So I put Samantha in the back seat and we went on a date...and that took care of that."

Hot Wheels

January 8, 1988

PINEVILLE, Ky. -- When the fire alarm sounds in the city of Pineville, 71-year-old volunteer fireman John Schwegler jumps on his 10-speed bicycle and takes off.

"I have no idea how fast I go," Schwegler said. "I've gone as fast as I could make it, considering the traffic, time of day and what is safe."

Schwegler, a retired mechanic, didn't learn to ride a bike until his first grandson was learning to ride a good many years ago.

He traded a baby bed for his first bicycle, but he now answers fire calls on a bike that a local cycle repairman built with parts from several other bicycles -- and that isn't fire-engine red, but metallic blue.

"When I first started riding a bicycle, everybody looked. But now, if I walk downtown, they want to know where the bicycle is," Schwegler said.

As pump engineer for the Pineville volunteer fire department, Schwegler, who joined the department in 1986, does not usually roll on car fires. But he does work gas spills, and sometimes he helps direct traffic at small fires around town.

"I know the town, and when I leave here, I go down the alley," Schwegler said. "So if you left here in a car right now, and me on that bicycle, you'd have a hard time beating me to the Shell service station down there."

Although Schwegler has no lights or siren on his bicycle, he says he is considering a dome light.

146

"There is a fire hat with a revolving light on top of it," Schwegler said. "My youngest grandson had one, and I don't know what he did with it, and I haven't seen one. When I see one, I'm going to buy it."

Schwegler says that, other than the chain jumping off the sprocket, he's never had a mishap with the bicycle.

"I watch, because when I'm out with it, I know that I'm on the losing end. You don't argue with cars, trucks or anything else. It wouldn't do me any good to start to a fire and wind up down here under a car somewhere."

This time of year, Schwegler, though busy with his sideline as a tax preparer, keeps his fire alarm beeper nearby.

"These close fires here, why about every time I go on my bicycle, I'll be there by the time, or before, the fire truck gets there," he said. "I mean, when that beeper goes off ...a lot of times, I'm on my bicycle -- waiting to see which direction I need to go -- by the time that thing quits beeping."

Pineville Fire Chief Billy Robbins and more than 20 other volunteers good-naturedly accept the bicycle, Schwegler said, but none of the others have bicycles.

"In fact," Schwegler said, "I don't know of a fireman anywhere else that rides a bicycle. But there may be some in some of these bigger cities that just haven't had the exposure that I have."

Death Valley Scotty

August 29, 1986

CYNTHIANA, Ky. -- Death Valley's most famous citizen, "Death Valley Scotty," is still as much a mystery in Cynthiana, his hometown, as in the California desert where he became legendary.

Some believed he was a con artist and charlatan; others theorized that he had found Death Valley's mother lode.

In either case, Walter E. Scott was a reporter's dream, a master showman whose wit and charming appearance made him an irresistible story subject.

Hank Johnston, in his book *Death Valley Scotty -- The Fastest Con in the West*, states that Scotty was born in Cynthiana "probably on Sept. 20, 1872." An accurate birth record could not be located, and Scotty's own account of his birth date often varied by several years.

Scotty was the youngest of six children, born to George A. and Anna Cahoun Scott, who lived on a farm 3 1/2 miles southwest of Cynthiana where the elder Scott raised and trained trotting horses, the biographer wrote.

Soon after Scotty was born, his mother died and his father married Susan Kate Wornall, a widow with four children.

His older brothers eventually migrated westward, where they found jobs as ranch hands. At about age 11, Scotty also left home to become a cowboy in Nevada.

Apparently he drifted from job to job, once with a 20-mule-team wagon train hauling Borax out of Death Valley, and, at one point, even as a stunt rider and sharpshooter with Buffalo Bill's Wild West Show. He got a job in a Colorado gold mine around 1900.

Johnston writes that Scotty's wife, a New York candy store clerk, was given two impressive chunks of gold ore by the mine superintendent during a visit to the mine shortly after her marriage to Scotty.

Some suspect Scotty later used the gold samples to gain financial backing from Julian M. Gerard, a prominent New York banker, for prospecting a mythical gold mine that he claimed to have discovered in Death Valley.

Scotty periodically wrote to the financier, assuring him that he was busy working the claim in the unbearable heat and asking for more money.

Gerard finally stopped sending money, but Scotty soon found another backer, Albert M. Johnson, a Chicago insurance executive. Johnson was quoted in Kenneth Alexander's "Death Valley U.S.A." as saying, "Scotty doesn't have a dime. I've been paying his bills for years. He repays me in laughs and I like him."

Written accounts of Scotty's life tell of one bizarre scheme after another; of renting a Santa Fe Railroad train with the agreement that he would pay the railroad $100,000 if the train could get him from Los Angeles to Chicago in 46 hours; of his story, in 1904, that he had been robbed of $12,000 in gold dust; and a tale in 1912 that he had sold his mine in the hills for $3 million.

Most Death Valley Scotty historians appear to agree that Johnson, even after recognizing Scotty's bogus claims of gold in Death Valley, was so taken by the character that he knowingly indulged in Scotty's grand ventures.

The crowning monument to Scotty's life of escapades is an edifice known as Scotty's Castle, still standing in Death Valley.

Built in the 1920s, with Johnson's money, the magnificent, Spanish-style stucco complex with more than 33,000 square feet of floor space and topped with a 56-foot-tall tower clock is now a tourist attraction in Death Valley National Park.

On a sun-parched hill overlooking the castle is the grave of Death Valley Scotty, who died in 1954 at the age of 81 -- give or take a few years.

Ross Hopkins, a National Park Service ranger at Death Valley, could offer no information as to what happened to Scotty's wife and son.

And in Cynthiana, where Scotty's life began, little is remembered of the famous character.

Some relatives of Scotty's stepmother, Susan Wornall, still live in the area, and a few have heard stories about him. But a telephone check of several people with the last name of Scott in Cynthiana failed to turn up a single one who had ever heard of Death Valley's most famous resident.

Hard Rock Cafe

March 10, 1986

LEXINGTON, Ky. -- Dr. Joe Daugherty may be the only man in Kentucky who can serve a lavish dinner made entirely with rocks.

Then, for your after-"dinner" amusement, he may take you on a guided tour of the rest of his rock

collection, highlighted by his displays of gallstones and kidney stones.

Daugherty, a professor at the University of Kentucky School of Dentistry who also has a private practice in Lexington, has been interested in rocks since his boyhood days on a Mercer County farm.

"The farm was fairly rocky, and when my older brother left home, he entrusted me with his little treasure chest of arrowheads that he had found on that place, a few of which I still have," he recalled.

Today, Daugherty's Lexington home is a veritable museum of natural and man-made oddities, from his fossil and fluorescent rock collection to a small Christmas tree decorated with human teeth. A tooth inlaid with a gold star is at the top; the blue ones are teeth from UK athletes who asked that they be painted blue.

His "rock dinner," which weighs more than 300 pounds, is the result of Daugherty's 17-year search for rocks that resemble food, either in shape or coloration.

Some rocks, such as his "old Kentucky ham" and his "baked potatoes," have been left as is. Others have been sliced with his rock saw and polished.

Among the many entrees are cauliflower, peas, lima beans, a lamb chop, beef steaks, ham steaks, roasts, a child's plate featuring rock burgers and rock fries, and even a tossed salad and a Coca-Cola made of rocks.

The roasts are garnished with parsley made from coral; the table is decorated with rock flowers.

For dessert, there is an attractive box of candy made from rocks, and after dinner there is even a rock cigar, with ashes from Mount St. Helens.

The unique collection has been featured on several popular network television shows, at a Minneapolis food convention and at numerous mineral society shows, fairs and art shows.

His extensive and unbelievable collection of gallstones and kidney stones, numbering in the hundreds, has been assembled over the past 15 years.

"I was working at Central Baptist Hospital one day in the pathology lab, and I noticed this multiplicity of what I call 'people rocks' in a big drawer," Daugherty said. "I inquired of the pathologist what he was going to do with them, and he said, 'Nothing,' so I told him I wanted them."

Since then, Daugherty said, he and a surgeon friend have been collecting gallstones and kidney stones from other hospitals in the Lexington area.

"Lately, an ultrasound device has been invented that will dissolve these things in people, without surgery, meaning that the day may come when there won't be any more," Daugherty remarked with a chuckle. "In that case, I'll be sitting on a cloud."

A mysterious greenish rock, referred to in some lapidary journals as "depalite," takes its name from Daugherty and three of his friends, named Ellis, Palmer and Anderson, who began finding the rocks about 15 years ago.

"Geologically, it hardly fits any specimen," Daugherty said. "It is of the chert family, a very broad classification. It appears to be found mostly in a few counties in Central Kentucky. Some of the better specimens are found in Powell, Estill and Montgomery counties.

"I am a rockhound," Daugherty confessed, scanning his backyard, cluttered with rocks. "My wife, Elizabeth, tolerates it. But I've promised to clean up some of this, later this year."

Bucking for Success

June 21, 1991

WINCHESTER, Ky. -- There's a lot more to being a professional rodeo cowboy than just riding a horse that bucks, Mike Stokley says, and he ought to know.

Stokley, 26, who has been riding the professional rodeo circuit since 1987, figures he was thrown the first time -- from the back of a calf -- in a barn lot in his native Clark County at about age 6.

"Later on, I used to get my grandpa's cows up in the apple orchard and buck them out into the pasture," he recalled.

When he was 15, Stokley began competing in open rodeos in Southern Kentucky and Tennessee, riding bulls and bareback broncs.

"I didn't want to ride saddle broncs, but about the second or third year I was rodeoing, some guy came up sick and they had a horse, and I said, 'Well, I'll just give it a try.' I started winning money, and I've liked it ever since," he said.

Stokley did not participate in sports in high school, but he earned a rodeo scholarship after winning the Ozark Region in bronc riding while a student of agriculture at Eastern Kentucky University, and in 1988 he was among the top 20 collegiate saddle bronc riders in the nation.

"I think it's just the challenge; kind of a natural high, like playing a good basketball game or a good game of golf," he explained.

Over the years he has accumulated a few scars and broken bones, a trademark among rodeo cowboys. He lost a finger team roping and has had two broken ankles, serious knee injuries and a whole bunch of sprains, pulls, cuts, bruises and concussions.

"I've had horses flip and I'd get concussions and not remember

153

anything," Stokley said. "I had a horse one time that I got hung up in a bareback rigging, and he was bucking down by a fence and bucked so high that he missed his front feet and turned a flip and caught my head on a gate."

Such incidents may be exciting for spectators, but they make life miserable for cowboys.

Stokley has a book filled with the names of dozens of horses that he has ridden since turning pro. In it he keeps a record of how much rein to give each horse, the patterns that the animal bucks and how the horse performs in different arenas.

He usually competes in about 40 rodeos each year, from Georgia and Alabama to Illinois, Iowa and Arkansas, and sometimes farther west.

"There are quite a few open rodeos in the state of Kentucky, but only one professional rodeo -- the circuit finals in Louisville for the Great Lakes Region (which takes in most of the states from South Dakota eastward and from Kentucky northward). There's a lot of professional rodeos in Ohio, Indiana, Illinois and Tennessee, and I've been in Missouri the last three weekends," Stokley said.

"I travel with some guys from Cincinnati, and some from the western part of Kentucky who are bull riders. And we just kind of hook up and pick two or three rodeos."

In order to be a top contender on the professional circuit, Stokley says that a rodeo cowboy needs to participate in about 100 rodeos a year and stay healthy. Stokley has ridden well enough to make it to the circuit finals in Louisville for the past four years.

"I get by, but I don't win as much as I'd like to," he said.

Life outside of professional rodeo is not that much different for Stokley, who, when not riding saddle broncs, divides his time between managing an 1,800-acre horse farm in Madison County and breaking thoroughbreds and quarter horses at a corral near his place east of Winchester.

He often rides as many as six unbroken horses every day.

"Last year I had the whole top part of my lip cut off -- 25 stitches -- when a horse I was breaking pawed me in the mouth, and then later I had a horse flip over backwards on me and laid me up for a good two months," Stokley said.

"It's more dangerous breaking horses than it is going to rodeos, because at a rodeo I know what to expect."

The Tyrone Bridge

March 10, 1989

TYRONE, Ky. -- "'You might call it Kentucky's best-kept secret,'" said Ralph Rasmussen, a 60-year-old retired mechanical engineer who lives in Brown City, Mich.

He was speaking of Young's High Bridge -- an abandoned Norfolk Southern Railroad bridge across the Kentucky River at Tyrone, between Anderson and Woodford counties. Rasmussen believes it is the last of its type in the United States.

"It is a single-span, deck-over cantilever," Rasmussen explained. "There is nothing like it that I know of in this country. I drove all the way down there back in January just to see it and to take pictures of it."

Cantilever bridges are built without piers in the middle; their center spans are held up only by pier-supported arms that extend from each shore.

A span called High Bridge, still in railroad use over the Kentucky River between Jessamine and Mercer counties, was built as a cantilever in 1876. But because of modifications over the years it is no longer a true cantilever, Rasmussen said.

He calls the design of Young's High Bridge, named for Bennett H. Young, a Confederate officer from Nicholasville, "probably the grandfather" of all modern cantilever bridges.

"Deck-over means that the road deck -- in this case the railroad deck -- is over the top, rather than through the steel structure," he said. "The Tyrone bridge is the quintessential cantilever."

155

After visiting the bridge, Rasmussen wrote the Kentucky Historical Society urging that something be done to save the historically significant structure for posterity.

He will be happy to learn that the bridge, which will be 100 years old in August, has not been forgotten.

William H. Johnson of Lexington, past president of the Bluegrass Railroad Museum, says his group is interested in acquiring and preserving the bridge; it bought 5.6 miles of the Norfolk Southern line two years ago.

"Right now, at worst, what would happen to it is that they would remove the rails and the cross ties, and wooden structure that could rot, and would leave the basic structure in place," Johnson said.

He added that there have been informal talks between the all-volunteer, not-for-profit museum -- which is near Versailles in Woodford County and about 5 1/2 miles east of the bridge -- and the management of Boulevard Distillers, which operates the Wild Turkey distillery on the Anderson County side of the river, about tying the museum's railroad excursions to a plant tour at the distillery.

Although the bridge -- 1,659 feet long and 281 feet over low-water level -- is structurally sound, Johnson says it would not support the weight of the heavy cars that his museum uses to move passengers.

"One of the things that has been bandied about informally is to maybe put a rail bus or a trolley, or something like that, over the bridge," that would run a shuttle from the distillery to the museum, Johnson said.

"Another thing that's been discussed has been the possibility of just decking and railing the bridge, and turning it into a pedestrian walkway and overlook."

It is not a bad idea, considering that Young's High Bridge has, for years, been a temptation for thrill-seekers and sightseers of all ages.

John Goodlett, who works at the distillery, says he often sees people walking on the bridge and has seen automobiles and motorcycles driven across it.

"Sometimes you'll see somebody walk out there and crawl back on all fours," he said. "They really get lively out there on the Fourth of July."

Mussel--Shell Memorials

November 27, 1989

STRAW, Ky. -- For many years, the Hill Grove Baptist Church cemetery in northeastern Edmonson County has been set apart from other country graveyards by the mussel-shell decorations of its mounded graves.

The shells cover nearly 100 graves in the cemetery beside the church, on a country road that ends at the edge of Nolin Lake.

While the shells atop the graves are a mystery to most outsiders, and even to some who live in the area, Elburtia Sanders, 76, who lives near the Hill Grove Church, says that the practice was begun at Hill Grove about 70 years ago by a woman named Ivy Decker, who lived in the area.

She says that Decker, who died several years back and is buried at Hill Grove, would gather mussel shells from Nolin River, boil them in lye to remove the dark outer-coating, then clean them until they were white and arrange them neatly on the tops of graves.

"Ivy just thought it up herself, and she's the one that got me started," Sanders said. "There was a cemetery down close to her house at Nolin Baptist Church, and she just fixed a few graves like that. Then she put them on my aunt's grave here at Hill Grove, and my sister's grave was next . . . and there just kept being more buried there."

Sanders says that she has been covering graves with mussel shells in the church cemetery since she was 8 or 9 and that each spring she and a daughter, some granddaughters and a neighbor clean and replace many of the shells.

"I just love to do it," Sanders said. "We fix about 65 graves every year, but there's a whole lot with shells on them that we don't clean off because the families do. The shells wear out and start breaking up every eight to ten years."

At one time, moss was gathered from the woods to cover the grave mounds before the shells were placed on top, but Sanders says that in recent years the moss has been replaced with synthetic turf.

"People from everywhere hear of the cemetery and come in here to see it," Sanders said. "There've even been people from New York ... and year before last, a woman from Florida was here and said she was going to put it in the paper down there."

Several natives of the northeastern Edmonson and southwestern Hart counties say they can recall scattered graves being decorated with mussel shells years ago, but Hill Grove is now thought to be among the few cemeteries in the area, if not the only one, where the custom is still widely practiced.

Sanders says that most of the mussel shells used on the graves are found in Nolin River and that it takes approximately two five-gallon buckets full of shells to cover one grave. She boils the shells in a 55-gallon drum filled with lye, then washes them and chips off the slate-colored exterior to prepare them for the grave decorations.

"I've got six girls and three granddaughters here, and after I'm gone, I think they'll all do it as long as they're able," she said.

"The last grave that was covered with shells was last summer on my sister's grave. We brought her from Leitchfield and buried her down here."

The Dueling Tree

January 25, 1993

GEORGETOWN, Ky. -- The "dueling tree" has finally lost its fight with time.

A large burr oak that stood for several centuries in a meadow beside a stream, just across the Scott County line from Fayette County, now lies splintered upon the same ground where several men fell beneath it during Kentucky's storied era of duels.

James Barton and his brother, Robert, who now own the farm on which the tree grew, adjacent to the Kentucky Horse Park, are uncertain of the tree's exact age but know it was among the rapidly dwindling number of large oaks that shaded tall-grass savannas around Central Kentucky when the first long hunters surveyed what now is known as the Bluegrass.

The land was for years the property of Gen. Basil Duke, whose brother-in-law, the celebrated Confederate Gen. John Hunt Morgan, often kept cavalry horses in barns at the Duke farm.

Historian J. Winston Coleman Jr., in his book *Famous Kentucky Duels*, called the spot where the tree stood "the favorite dueling grounds of central Kentucky." While the tree itself may not have been of much significance to duelers, its proximity to the county line increased the difficulty of proving in which county the duel had been fought.

Possibly the first duel at the site was in the summer of 1818 -- between two young Lexington physicians, Benjamin W. Dudley and William H. Richardson. Originally, the dispute was between Dudley and a friend of Richardson's over the autopsy of a man who died after a drunken brawl. But when his friend declined the challenge to duel, Richardson accepted in his stead.

The two men, accompanied by their attendants, met at the site, bowed to each other and flipped a coin for the choice of position and the right to give the word. They took their places facing one another at 10 paces and fired at command. When the smoke cleared, Dudley was untouched but Richardson lay badly wounded, and might have died had Dudley not worked to save his life.

Despite anti-dueling meetings and legislative concern about the Southern gentleman's deadly way of settling differences, duels continued for many years.

In 1829 another famous duel took place near where the old burr oak stood. This duel was between Robert Wickliffe, for many years a state senator from Lexington, and George Trotter, a young newspaper editor from Lexington, whose paper had made disparaging remarks about Wickliffe. Trotter escaped without a scratch; Wickliffe was mortally wounded.

In 1848, William O. Smith of Paris, Ky., and Thomas H. Holt of St. Louis reportedly fired several shots at each other -- though neither was hit -- then managed to settle their differences without bloodshed.

Formal duels were on the decline in Kentucky by the end of the Civil War, but the 1866 duel between Joseph Desha and Alexander Kimbrough, both of Harrison County, who had served on different sides in the war, was among the best-remembered duels to have been fought near the oak.

Using pistols that had belonged to Henry Clay, himself a duelist, the two men faced off at 30 feet, fired and missed. But on the second firing, Kimbrough, who had served as a sergeant in the Union Army, received a wound that troubled him the rest of his life. Desha, who had been a Confederate captain, escaped the duel unmarked, except for a bullet hole in his coat pocket.

No duels have known to have been fought at the oak thereafter.

Just before Christmas 1992, as Kentucky's bicentennial year drew to a close, the dueling tree crashed to the ground one night in a windstorm.

James Barton says his family hopes to salvage a few pieces of usable lumber from the fallen landmark, and perhaps one day make a keepsake piece of furniture from the magnificent tree around which so much of Kentucky's history unfolded.

Brushed by History

October 3, 1988

JUNCTION CITY, Ky. -- In the late hours of Oct. 29, 1921, a rabid fan of Centre College's "Praying Colonels" football team -- jubilant over the Danville school's defeat of Harvard University that day -- armed himself with paint and a brush and scrawled the score on the corner of Burke's Bakery in Junction City.

"CENTRE-6, HARVARD-0."

LaRue Burke, 87, of Lexington, whose father owned the bakery at the time, says the "painter" was the late George Allery Blacketer, known to folks around Junction as "Babe."

"He usually did most of his work at night," Burke said of Blacketer.

"Nobody knew who did it, but he confided in me that he did it. I think he used white paint, and my dad just let it stay there, because the building was just plain brick when my dad was there, and I guess he didn't want to paint the whole building."

Years later, the building was painted, but someone always repainted the score over the fresh paint, and at some point, CENTRE came to be spelled incorrectly, with an E-R instead of an R-E.

Spelling notwithstanding, the score on the corner of the old building, on Junction City's Main Street about two miles south of Centre, has survived to become a perpetual reminder of one of the college's most glorious days.

"I remember when they telegrammed back and said they'd beaten Harvard, the town went crazy," recalled Ralph Cress of Danville, who was 5 years old at the time. "The score was painted all over town the next morning -- Centre-6, Harvard-0."

Reflecting on the significance of the victory, history must mercifully excuse the vandalism.

Centre, with an enrollment of about 200, a football field carved out of a pasture and a stadium that reportedly would seat about 1,000, met the Harvard Crimson in a great horseshoe stadium at Cambridge, Mass., jammed with 50,000 spectators.

Harvard had not been beaten in five years and, despite a tie with Penn State that season, had defeated Georgia, Boston University, Middlebury, Holy Cross and Indiana.

Centre had defeated Clemson, Virginia Polytechnic Institute, St. Xavier of Cincinnati and Transylvania.

Just a few days before the contest, the Boston Transcript said, "The game with the Kentuckians hardly will be more than an incident for Harvard, as during the next fortnight every effort will be made on preparing the team for the Princeton contest Nov. 5."

Incident indeed!

In their famous "Penitentiary Shift" formation -- so named because the linemen and backs tailing one another reminded some observers of prisoners marching in a line -- the Praying Colonels bedeviled Harvard's defense.

The only score of the bruising encounter was a 32-yard gallop by All-America Alvin "Bo" McMillan, who followed All-America James "Red" Roberts through the Harvard line to their right.

A Boston Globe account said that Roberts had spilled three men and was looking for more when McMillan reversed to his left and ran for the corner of the field.

It was a grand day for intercollegiate football, for Kentucky, Danville and Centre.

It was a grand day, too, for Junction City, a little railroad town just down the tracks from Centre that has never let the world forget the score.

While public reminders of Centre's victory eventually disappeared from buildings in Danville, Junction City's has survived. And some believe it may be the last one in Boyle county.

No one is sure exactly how many times the building in Junction City has been painted and the score replaced, but Betty Beck of Danville, the building's current owner, said her late brother, Chester Sheperson, its former owner, was the last one to paint the score, a few years ago.

"People would come there from everywhere to look at it when my brother owned it," she said.

Just last week, the building, which now contains several apartments, was painted again and the score obliterated. But Beck promises that it will be replaced, exactly where it was.

Oh yes, Centre will still be spelled C-E-N-T-E-R, as in CENTER-6, HARVARD-0.

Bandboozled

June 6, 1988

Have you heard about the time the Cole Bros. Circus was stolen in Scottsville, Ky.?

I hadn't, until I crossed paths with Jim Nichols, a Bowling Green banker who grew up in Allen County and who passed the story on to me one night while we were swapping yarns at Barren River.

The story has circulated around Scottsville since the incident occurred, sometime around 1880, and although some versions differ slightly, the basics remain the same.

It all started when a bunch of boys from Scottsville -- 15 of them, maybe, mostly in their late teens -- had a few drinks and went to the circus grounds one Saturday night while the Cole Bros. show was in town.

"When they got to the circus, the band was in the main tent, getting warmed up. About half the boys got on one side of the tent, and half on the other," as Nichols, 63, has heard it. "At a given signal, one group cut the ropes, and of course the tent started falling and pandemonium broke loose. The other half went in the tent and stole all the band instruments."

Paul Dalton, 80, of Scottsville, whose grandfather, the late Jimmy Gilmore, was in on the heist, says he's heard that the circus was broke and couldn't get out of Scottsville at the time. He was told that some of the boys actually got on stage and did some performing -- somersaults, handstands, etc. -- before making off with the instruments and an elephant.

Yes, all accounts of the story include an elephant.

"One thing led to another, and they decided they should have a parade," Nichols said. "So they took the elephant and some of the other animals, and a wagon and the band instruments, and started out uptown, around the courthouse.

"Two or three brothers in the group decided that their Pap, who was bedridden, hadn't seen an elephant in quite a few years, so they took the elephant home with them and had him up on the front porch, trying to get him in the house, when I guess they finally began to sober up a bit."

164

It is a shame that some of the participants in the incident did not later write a full account of what happened. It would be nice to know such details as what song the drunken band attempted to play as it marched through Scottsville, tooting stolen tubas and trombones, following a stolen elephant, or what the boys' sickly father said when he saw an elephant at the door.

Perhaps someone did leave a written record, but it is doubtful that they much wanted to remember stealing the circus, since there were numerous men in the group who later made names for themselves in various professions, including the practice of law.

The elephant and whatever other animals had been confiscated for the parade were eventually recovered, but the musical instruments stayed in Scottsville, where they were the nucleus of a town band that was quite celebrated in its day.

Today, on the wall in the Allen County library, there hangs a picture of the band, some of whose 15 to 20 members are holding instruments taken from the circus. A few of the instruments are known to still be in Scottsville.

It's not believed anyone went to jail for stealing the circus, but Dalton, a retired teacher and postal worker, says restitution was made for the instruments that were taken.

"The county court clerk at that time decided to uphold the honor of the town, and he raised enough money to pay the circus what money they were out for instruments," Dalton said. "The president of the circus later sent him a letter, telling him that the publicity they got from all that had happened enabled the circus to get back on its feet again."

Buffaloed

October 17, 1988

BLOOMFIELD, KY. -- Kentucky's resident cowboy, Jerry Hahn, may have finally met his match.

Hahn -- who rounds up wild cattle for $100 a head, who once had his own donkey baseball team, who broke a Texas longhorn steer and a Charolais bull to ride in parades, who tamed an eight-point buck to lead -- says he has never run up against anything as tough as the young bison that he now is trying to break to ride.

"The first thing he did was take me through four strands of barbed wire," Hahn said. "That was when I first got him, about seven months ago, when he was about six months old."

"He tore a brand new pair of pants off of me, and I went to the house one day just in my shorts. It's not funny. I had a new shirt, just like this. . . and he got his horn in the buttons, I guess, and stripped it off of me."

In addition, Hahn says, the young bison -- which he estimates weighs about 600 pounds -- has dislocated his shoulder, mashed his big toe and "skinned my legs up pretty bad."

Hahn and his father, Chester, on whose Nelson County farm the bison grazes, say that the animal isn't fazed by electric fences, that he can jump stiff-legged with all four feet off the ground at the same time, and that his occasional deep grunts are enough to make your hair stand on end.

Hahn got the idea to train the bison -- popularly called a buffalo -- when he saw a man riding one in a television commercial several months ago.

"I figured if he could do it, why couldn't I?" said Hahn, who hauls rock, trades livestock and serves part time as a special deputy sheriff in Nelson County.

But Hahn soon learned that the young animal he bought from a buffalo farm near Horse Cave, Ky., was nothing like those he had previously broken to ride.

"A horse or anything will finally tame down and you can handle them, the gentler you are," Hahn said. "That old longhorn steer I broke, for a week there, he was bad, but after that he calmed down.

"This buffalo, I've never been astraddle of his back . . . The only time I was ever close to his back was one day when he had me down and was astraddle of me."

Hahn looked down at the fresh tear in the sleeve of his hooded sweat shirt, then at the bundle of dynamite wrapped in hair, horns and hooves that he had spent 30 minutes wrestling out of the barn for a picture.

What's the buffalo's name?

"Do you mean what do I call him, or his real name?" Hahn asked. "He's got three of four names when he's dragging me up through the field, but Id rather not call any of them. Just give him a name," he said. "If I ever get him broke to a cart, I'll promise you it's no telling how many miles we can go in a short few seconds, 'cause he can move."

"If you get close to him, you can tell, in the top of your mind, a little bit which way he's going to go. But if you stay away from him, he'll knock you down, then he'll just tromp on you."

Hahn hasn't given up yet, but he is beginning to wonder what he should try next. His advice for others who might want to break a buffalo to ride: "Come and talk to me . . . 'cause it's rough."

Locust Tree

October 10, 1990

JUNCTION CITY, Ky. -- Lanny Coulter doesn't blame his friends for not believing his story about a black locust tree in a thicket on the edge of Junction City in Boyle County.

"I wouldn't believe it either, if you told me, so I don't blame you for not believing me. But it's the truth," the 39-year-old Southern Railway brakeman said.

Nearly 30 years ago, Coulter declares, the tree was nothing but a light pole, about 15 to 20 feet tall and some 6 to 8 inches in diameter.

He and his older brother and their father sawed it down -- a foot or two above the ground -- with a crosscut saw, about 1965, he said. They didn't remove the bark, but trimmed the limbs and twigs off, dragged it about a quarter-mile home with a horse, set the pole in a posthole 3 to 4 feet deep, then strung an electrical line on it leading from the house to his father's shop.

"I don't remember whether it sprouted right after we set it back or the next spring," Coulter said. "Daddy just broke the lower sprouts off, so he could get in the door (of the shop) and we just thought they'd all die out. But they just kept coming back." Today, the black locust appears perfectly healthy, and is about 15 inches in diameter and 40 feet tall.

The old Coulter place is all gone now, but the locust tree still has two ends of an electrical line hooked onto clamps, protruding a few inches from its forks -- 10 to 12 feet off the ground.

"I've seen plenty of posts, set in fence rows, that would sprout, and you'd come back the next year and break them off, but this is a *tree*," Coulter said.

His buddies on the railroad have been giving him a hard way to go over the tree. Some of them are calling him "Locust Tree Lanny."

One of them told of building a one-room cabin in the hills about 20 years ago, and how he had gone back the other day to discover that it had grown into a "log mansion."

Another wise guy suggested that Southern Railway could cut Coulter's locust, make toothpicks out of it, then plant them and grow its own cross ties.

Cary Perkins, chief of forest management for the Kentucky Division of Forestry, says that although he has never seen a locust post grow into a tree after being sawed off top and bottom, he believes it is possible.

Some trees have dormant buds in the bark that make them sprout and take root, even if the taproot is missing, he says. Even so, Perkins notes that a utility pole growing into a 40-foot-tall tree is rather unusual.

Meantime, Coulter has considered taking matters into his own hands in order to silence the skeptics. "I've told them if they'd bet me enough money, I'd come over here with a grubbing hoe and dig a hole down, and show them where it was cut off at the bottom," he said.

Remembering Lum 'n' Abner

May 24, 1991

LEXINGTON, Ky. -- Lum 'n' Abner's Jot'em Down Store may not mean much to anyone under age 55, but in the golden days of radio -- the 1930s and '40s -- Lum 'n' Abner were the country versions of Amos 'n' Andy.

The show originated in 1931 on radio station KTHS in Hot Springs, Ark., but it grew so popular that it lasted for 24 seasons on the ABC, CBS, NBC and Mutual Radio networks.

It was set in the fictional country town of Pine Ridge, Ark. -- which later became real when a small Arkansas town changed its name to Pine Ridge.

Lum 'n' Abner's partnership business -- the Jot'em Down Store -- was not only the seat of cracker barrel philosophy, but the birthplace of many big ideas.

One day Lum wanted to be a banker; the next day he was reading a "manualscript" for a great novel he hoped to publish on the printing press that he and Abner operated in the back of the store.

"I doggies, they's a limit to how much work a feller can do in one day," Abner would whine. "Special a little short feller like me."

After most of two decades on radio, the Jot'em Down Store closed when television arrived in the early 1950s, but Lum 'n' Abner's memory stays alive in a real Jot'em Down Store to which they passed on the name more than a half-century ago in the heart of Kentucky's horse country -- at the junctions of Russell Cave Pike and Iron Works Pike in northern Fayette County.

Bob Terrell, 62, the store's owner, says when he was a kid the store was called Terrell's General Store. Then one day, at the height of their stardom, Lum and Abner visited the place and changed things forever.

"My father, L.C. Terrell, and my Uncle Ed were running the store then, listening to the program, and they got to calling everybody around here by nicknames of people in the program," he said. "The guy that lived up the road was Mousie, and a man that lived down here was Grandpappy Spears, and a fella down there was Cedric, and Wehunt and so forth."

About 1937, Terrell says, Lum and Abner came through Fayette County buying horses. Someone told them about Terrell's store, and they stopped to see the place.

"They went to town and had a sign made that said, 'Jot'em Down Store,' " Terrell said.

He still has the original sign in the garage, and the store's name has remained "Jot'em Down."

Lum and Abner -- whose real names were Chester Lauck and Norris Goff -- left some autographed pictures of themselves at the store, and had some pictures made of Terrell's father and uncle, playing checkers, just as Lum 'n' Abner often did in their make-believe Jot'em Down Store.

The pictures are all still hanging on a pegboard in the rear of the store, near the sandwich counter.

Terrell says that Lum stopped in again several years ago, but he does not know what has happened to the two radio stars.

According to their ages listed in old news accounts, Abner would be about 85 today and Lum would be about 94.

Both would no doubt be pleased that Bob Terrell keeps a few tapes of their radio shows to play for tourists who sometimes stop by the Kentucky Jot'em Down Store and want to hear the tale of how it was named.

Fayette's Jot 'em Down Store

Milk Run

May 3, 1991

PARIS, Ky. -- Thousands of sightseers have streamed through the gates of Claiborne Farm over the years, hoping to glimpse the legendary horses who have lived there -- Secretariat, Bold Ruler, Spectacular Bid, Nasrulla, Ferdinand, Forty-Niner and Easy Goer, to name a few.

But there is another important animal at Claiborne that most visitors never see: Mrs. Hancock's cow, a 7-year-old Jersey whose milk provides cream for the kitchen of Waddel Hancock, matriarch of the 3,481-acre Bourbon County thoroughbred empire.

"I'm not bragging about the cow, but I don't know anybody who has a cow that gives cream like that," Mrs. Hancock declared. "I'm the one who insists on having the cow. That cream is out of this world. I'd as soon not eat cereal if I didn't have that cream on it."

Twice a day, a farm employee milks the Jersey by hand and takes the milk to the house, where it is run through a cream separator and given to Mrs. Hancock.

"We make butter, but we have an electric churn (if you want to know the truth) and we're doing well to get somebody to use that," Mrs. Hancock said.

"My friends sometimes want me to save them some cream for such and such an occasion, and it's a treat for me to be able to give it to them. But if I'm going to eat it myself, I just tell them I don't have any extra."

When first asked about the cow, Mrs. Hancock was a bit reluctant to discuss the animal, noting that Claiborne has built its reputation

172

on horses, not milk cows, and that she certainly did not want to "exploit the cow." She emphatically denied that the cow is a pet.

"I wouldn't know that cow if I'd see her somewhere," Mrs. Hancock said. "If she has a name, I don't know what it is."

Officially, the cow is named Daisy, but most call her "Mrs. Hancock's Cow," which is plenty name enough around Claiborne Farm.

"I could milk a cow when I was little," Mrs. Hancock recalled. "I used to go spend the summer at my grandmother's farm, and that was one of the special treats, that they'd let me milk a cow.

"I've had a cow ever since I was married," she said. "My mother-in-law had this delicious cream, and I'd never tasted any so good ...and I just thought, 'Well I'm going to have that myself, all my life,' and I have."

Her husband, A.B. Hancock Jr., who died in 1972, never paid much attention to the cow, she said, but he loved the cream.

In nice weather, Daisy spends most of her time grazing, virtually unnoticed, in a lot scarcely 100 yards from the stallion barn where Easy Goer lives. She is one in a long line of Jerseys who have spent their lives at Claiborne, providing cream for the Hancock table.

"I don't cook much myself, I'll be honest with you," Mrs. Hancock said, "but I'm not going to starve either.

"When I grew up, my mother told me, 'Don't ever learn how to cook, then you won't have to.' "

Russell Hudson

April 17, 1991

LIBERTY, Ky. -- Nearly every morning about sunup for the past 21 years, Russell Hudson has been unfurling Old Glory over the town of Liberty.

No pay or encouragement was ever necessary. Hudson, 86, considered it a privilege. It gave him a good feeling "some way or another," he says.

Rarely did anyone even notice when he arrived every morning, on foot, and again every afternoon about 5 to take the flag down, fold it neatly and carry it home, three blocks away, tucked under his arm.

His eyesight was so severely damaged by a childhood illness that he was never able to drive a car. He memorized an eye chart, lied about his age and joined the U.S. Army when he was 17, in 1922. For seven years he served as an infantryman and a bugler.

He still keeps a bugle hanging on his kitchen wall, and uses it to sound taps for the military funerals in which he participates with a funeral detail comprised of veterans.

"You want to hear it?" he asked.

He stood in the corner of his kitchen, as erect as his stooped shoulders would permit, put the horn to his lips and blew those sad, chilling notes that bring tears to the eyes of old soldiers.

"I've seen them fall a many a time while I was playing that," Hudson said. "I guess I've done 1,500 funerals; started way back yonder before World War II. I practice of a night here, but nobody hears me."

Occasionally, families of deceased veterans at whose funerals he plays give Hudson the flags from the caskets so he can fly them over Liberty.

"If a veteran dies, the way you do -- if he died last night and you know it this morning -- you go down there and run your flag to full staff, then pull it to half mast," Hudson explained, his voice breaking.

"I can't understand a man that enjoys freedom here being able to stomp a flag and burn it and everything else. Only a moron, I reckon, would do that."

For the past 35 years Hudson has been helping veterans fill out disability claims for the Veterans Administration. The work is voluntary and he does it "just to have something to do," the retired country postmaster says.

Hudson's wife died a few years ago, and he lives alone with his bugle, a few flags and some memories.

One day last fall -- hardly able to get out of bed because of painful arthritis -- Hudson was forced to give up raising the flag and turn the duties over to the caretaker at the courthouse.

He still hopes that on days when he can get around, he can go to the courthouse now and then, hoist the flag, then stand for a moment and watch her catch the breeze one more time.

He will miss her, but he need not fret about Old Glory. She waves forever for men like Russell Hudson.

Building Memories

December 13, 1991

HOPKINSVILLE, Ky.-- Gathial W. Knight's sorrow over the loss of his family's farm led him to find a gentle way of remembering.

The detailed miniature replicas that he made of the buildings on the farm quickly caught the eye of others who wanted their own favorite farm

buildings preserved in miniature. And what began as a pastime for a down-on-his-luck farmer now promises to become a profitable hobby.

Knight, 40, still finds it painful to discuss the loss of the Christian County farm where he was raised, and where he and his father were partners until his father's death in 1981, at the age of 61.

That, he says, is when things began to fall apart.

Knight is one of eight children, and because his father left no will, the 400-acre farm had to be sold to settle the estate. Knight could not afford to buy the place, and in 1983, he and his wife, Cathy, and their two children (they have since had a third) watched helplessly as their home, farm and most of the equipment was sold at auction.

"People say, 'Well, farming is just a job.' No, *family* farming is not just a job, it's a way of life, and it's in you," Knight said. "Even two or three years after my dad passed away, I'd look up across a field on the farm and he'd be there ... especially when I'd see something that we'd done together; something that we'd patched or worked on.

"And after my mother passed away in '83, I could walk around that farm over there and see her. She'd help us in the tobacco patch all day ...and she loved flowers. And I could see her out there fighting crab grass in the garden."

Knight now has a job mowing highway rights of way and working as a mechanic for the state highway garage in Christian County, but he still holds a deep attachment to the family farm, and the miniature buildings he makes in his free time have helped him stay in touch with the way of life he misses.

"It takes my mind off everything else, trying to get the detail," Knight said. "They're not prefabricated. I'm tired of that kind of stuff."

Although barns are his primary interest, his miniature farm buildings run the gamut, from farmhouses to corn cribs, smoke houses to coal houses, tool sheds to chicken coops.

Most of his replicas are made with wooden swizzle sticks and skewers. Some of the barns have hinged doors, stalls, hay racks, lofts, ladders, gear rooms, loading chutes and other interior fixtures. Simulated tin roofs are made of heavy tin foil; those resembling wood shingles are made by layering the ends of the swizzle sticks.

Prices for the buildings -- most of which are 6 to 8 inches tall -- range from about $30 for basic shells to $75 or more for detailed, custom-made replicas of farm buildings, which often require more than 40 hours of work.

Knight has made about 70 pieces since he built a machine shed for his 4-year-old son, Trevor, in January 1990. He currently is building a large, turn-of-the-century mule barn and has several orders on a waiting list.

His father-in-law, Bill Helzer, an artist, helps him paint the buildings, including the barns, which have a weathered look.

"One man got me to build an old stable, and he wanted to paint 'See Rock City' on the roof," Knight said. "If a person gives me a sketch or a picture of what they want, the front, each side and the back, and what they want inside, I can build it fairly close.

"Several people have told me that they didn't think I could do anything like this. I tell them it's just luck ...and I've been waiting a long time."

Looking for a Sign

October 9, 1990

An unusual project aimed at locating dozens of 19th-century boundary markers on the Kentucky-Tennessee line is being undertaken by surveyors from the two states.

A joint committee of the Kentucky and Tennessee associations of professional surveyors has volunteered to try to find and catalog the remnants of 63 limestone monuments that were set along the boundary when the line was surveyed by a joint commission of the two states in 1858-59. They have found about 15 of the markers so far.

The boundary -- which once divided the colonies of North Carolina and Virginia -- is steeped in history, having been the subject of much controversy in colonial days and, later, between Tennessee and Kentucky.

Andrew Kellie, a Murray State University engineering professor and an authority on the history of the line, said the portion of it that's east of the Tennessee River was accepted as the boundary by the legislatures of Tennessee and Kentucky in 1820.

However, Kellie noted that the original survey of that part of the line, done by Dr. Thomas Walker in 1779, is probably about 16 miles too far north.

"By that time, Walker was in his 60s," Kellie said. "He was surveying land that was contested by a couple of Indian tribes. He had had a disagreement with the North Carolina commissioners, and, in fact, prior to getting to what is now the south-eastern corner of Kentucky at Cumberland Gap, the two boundary commissions had actually run two separate boundary lines between North Carolina and Virginia."

178

The North Carolinians refused to work with Walker and left him to continue west, through rugged and sometimes hostile territory, without their assistance. The circumstances were not conducive to a good survey.

"I think if you were to trace the parallel on the ground that is supposed to be the southern boundary of Kentucky -- the original line of the North Carolina Charter -- it would be south of where it is today by about 16 miles," Kellie said.

Generally speaking, such a line would parallel the southern boundary of Kentucky's Jackson Purchase region (which was correctly surveyed later) on a latitude due east, and would, Kellie said, put all of Clarksville, Tenn. -- a city of about 75,000 people -- in Kentucky, along with many smaller Tennessee towns.

The current joint committee of surveyors from each state, of which Kellie is a member, has no intention of rekindling debate over the boundary. It intends only to identify and record the historic markers placed in 1858 and 1859, many of which may still exist.

"I think the benefit to come out of this is that the importance of the boundary is emphasized, and public awareness is called to the fact that there is a line on the ground that separates the two states, and separates one person's land from another, and that the boundary line should be preserved and the monuments honored," Kellie said.

Using the field notes of the surveyors who marked the line in the 1850s, the modern-day surveyors will try, over the next two years, to locate all of the 63 old monuments. Each was numbered, and each has the abbreviations "KY" and "TENN" chiseled on the appropriate side, with the date.

Surveyor James R. Adams of Bowling Green, Ky., thinks the limestone for the monuments was quarried in Warren County. The monuments are about a foot square at the top and a foot and a half square at the base, and they weigh a few hundred pounds.

"They're sunk about 3 or 4 feet in the ground, and they stick out of the ground about 2 feet," Adams said. "The ones that we find, we're going to take pictures of, and rubbings, and actually locate in the field, and write a description of how to get to them."

There are no plans to replace the missing markers, or to move existing ones, beyond setting them upright or recovering them if they have been uprooted by excavation or vandalism, Adams said.

Choctaw Academy

September 23, 1981

GEORGETOWN, Ky. -- The rolling farmland of Scott County seems a most unlikely place for an Indian academy. Yet it was here, in 1825, that such an academy was founded.

Why?

I have yet to find a simple answer. But it is known that Baptists in America experienced a wave of missionary zeal shortly before the school was established, and that the Elkhorn Association of Baptists in Kentucky had, in 1801, ordained a man named John Young as a missionary to the Indians.

Furthermore, it is believed that missionaries to the Indian nations were having problems managing the mission schools, and that some Indian leaders concluded that a school "placed at some distance from the nation" might be the best solution to removing the boys from the indulgence of parents.

It so happened that Col. Richard M. Johnson of Scott County offered his farm and facilities for the school.

Johnson, his father and his brother were all active in the Elkhorn Baptist Association, and Col. Johnson enjoyed a wide reputation as a politician and builder. He is credited by some historians with having killed Indian chief Tecumseh, at the battle of the River Thames, and he served as vice-president during the Van Buren administration.

In early 1823 the Choctaw nation and the U.S. government entered into a treaty providing $6,000 a year for 20 years for the education of Choctaw children.

In the fall of that year, 21 young Choctaws arrived at Col. Johnson's Blue Spring Farm west of Georgetown to begin school.

In the 1928 "Chronicles of Oklahoma," a quarterly publication of the Oklahoma historical Society historian Carolyn Thomas Foreman listed each of those first pupils, and his age . . . from Morris Nail, who was 8, to Alfred Wade, 17.

Scattered in between were Jacob Folsom, 16; Silas Pitchlynn, 15; William Riddle, 14; Charles King, 13; Picken Wade, 12; and many others.

Although the names may not sound Indian, it is a fact that Folsoms and Pitchlynns were names in the Choctaw hierarchy.

Indeed, it seems that a large number of Indian boys who attended the school where of Indian aristocracy. Jacob LeFlore, a student there in 1820, was the son of Choctaw Chief Greenwood LeFlore.

And there soon came students from many tribes other than the Choctaws; from the Miami, Seminole, Quapaw and Cherokee nations, from the Creek, Chickasaw, Potawatami, Shawnee and Osage.

Chickasaw Chief Lewis Colbert sent his son, Dougherty, to study at the academy. Shawnee Chief Anthony Chein's son, Charles, was also a student.

There were five buildings on the school grounds, the academy itself being a two-story stone house 40 by 24 feet, according to Ann Bevins' "A History of Scott County As Told By Selected Buildings." The three other stone buildings were used for dining and lodging. There was one frame structure.

Col. Johnson selected the Rev. Thomas Henderson as superintendent of the academy, describing him as "a man of uncommon merit, a scientific character with globes, a preacher of the Gospel, eminent for his literary talents and his amiable disposition, a man of business, industrious, dignified and conciliatory in his manners."

And what of the students?

Henderson's first quarterly report to Washington, on January 31, 1826, said, "The boys are lively and cheerful, peaceable and well disposed, easily governed and ambitious to excel.

"I have not had occasion to chastise any of them yet, nor indeed, but seldom to call any to account for misconduct. My method is when occasion requires it, in the most determined and solemn manner talk to the offender in the presence of the whole school calling them my sons, and in the most tender and affectionate manner point out the evil consequences resulting from bad conduct and a disregard to order; and the benefits resulting from good behavior.

"In some of the lectures I have seen the tears flow freely."

Students at the school studied bookkeeping, astronomy and some surveying, in addition to wagon-making, farming and tannery.

Henderson kept notes about the progress of each student, by tribe, and the "Chronicles of Oklahoma" (on file at the Kentucky Historical Society Library in Frankfort) contain such observations as these:

"Jarratt Bee (?) . . . 18 . . . Cherokees . . . Good Mind.

George Ross . . . 16 . . . Cherokees . . . Ordinary . . .

Wm. Cass . . . 14 . . . Miames . . . Good Mind . . .

Jos. Rushaville . . . Miames . . . 16 . . . Dull . . ."

In 1831 the school was moved a few miles away to White Sulphur Spring, still located on property owned by Col. Johnson.

Two years later, in 1833, a cholera epidemic struck the school. Many doctors were called in, but nine of the young students died.

The 20-year agreement providing government funding for the academy expired in 1845. Some histories say that the academy closed in 1843 because of declining enrollment.

All that remains today is one of the stone buildings at the original site of the school, near Blue Spring in western Scott County.

The farm is owned by Mrs. Joe H. Gaines of Georgetown. I am indebted to Mrs. Gaines' grandson, Rodes Kelly, to Anthony Lewis of Indianapolis, a relation of Superintendent Thomas Henderson, and to Linda Anderson of the Kentucky Historical Society Library for their invaluable assistance in helping me recall this unusual chapter in Kentucky's past.

Accidental Petroleum
September 18, 1989

YAMACRAW, Ky. -- At the edge of a remote logging road, hemmed in by the Big South Fork of the Cumberland River and the rugged mountains of southwestern McCreary County, there is an old oil well, nearly hidden in the underbrush.

No marker is at the site, no date on the cap, nothing to suggest that this well is any different from the hundreds of other forgotten wells drilled and capped along the Kentucky-Tennessee border.

Yet this well -- drilled in 1818 -- holds the distinction of being the first commercial oil well in the United States.

The drillers, Marcus Huling and his partner, Andrew Zimmerman, were searching for salt on a farm owned by Martin Beatty when they struck the "devil's tar," as it was known in those days.

Salt being far more valuable than oil at the time, the strike did not occasion much celebration.

In fact, history records that, after the oil overflowed the well, seeping into what is today named Oil Well Branch, then into the Big South Fork, it created what probably was the first oil slick in Kentucky, incurring the wrath of a local farmer whose geese were coated with the stuff.

Huling is said to have been threatened and shot at and his oil spills set ablaze by angry farmers. And he nearly drowned when he tried to float the oil out in barrels through the treacherous rapids known as "Devil's Jump," about six miles downstream.

Eventually, with the help of mules and horses, Huling was able to move small quantities of his oil out of the steep hills and market it to the outside world.

In an 1820 letter to his brother, David, who lived in Lewistown, Pa., Huling said he had sold 2,000 gallons of oil to Europe, where it was used to make liniment and other cure-alls, and that some 100 gallons had been taken to North Carolina and Georgia. James Holmberg, curator of manuscripts for Louisville's Filson Club, which has the letter, says that Huling indicated to his brother that there was a serious dispute over the land on which the South Fork well was located, that he had made no salt there, and that he was in much need of money.

McCreary author and historian Samuel D. Perry, in his book, "South Fork Country," says that it was in that same year that Huling, his reputation, popularity and money all gone, decided he had been in the oil business long enough and moved on to other parts of rural Kentucky, still in search of salt.

Zimmerman apparently had forsaken the costly, ill-fated venture much earlier.

Numerous other names would be associated with the early marketing of oil, but most of them not before the late 1820s, well after Huling had capped and abandoned his well.

Reminders of Huling's efforts are found in the museum in nearby Stearns where there is on display a heavy old iron drill bit that someone found near the old well. And in a display case nearby is a small jar of crude, dipped from the historic well several years ago. It was 1970 before the Kentucky General Assembly passed a resolution honoring Huling, Zimmerman and Martin Beatty for their efforts as early petroleum producers and marketers.

It urged that the Kentucky Department of Public Information place the location of the historic well on its travel maps, and that the Kentucky Historical Society place a marker commemorating the site.

The marker now stands on the lawn of the McCreary County Courthouse in Whitley City.

Blind Mystic

February 8, 1989

CINCINNATI -- For years many people in west-central Kentucky knew Clintie Morris as "the blind mystic." They traveled miles to seek his counsel about their futures, and his help in finding lost objects or loved ones.

When Morris was born 93 years ago next month there were complications, and no doctor was available for several hours. As a result, Morris was blind.

It is thought that he was born in Harlan County, but he spent most of his early years in the Cub Run section of Hart County, and he later lived in Hardin County. For about the past 25 years he has been in nursing homes.

He was in his 20s, he says, when he began to realize that he could see beyond his blindness into a mysterious realm that defied even his own explanation.

"My mother went visiting one day, and when she got home, I told her what she had talked about and what she had seen while she was gone. Even told her how she'd seen turkeys on the side of the road," Morris recalled.

"She said, 'He's a fortune teller.' "

Word of Morris' strange talent soon began to spread, and visitors -- sometimes as many as 25 or more a day -- came to him with questions.

"They'd come to me from different places -- some clear from Texas," he recalled during an interview a few days ago at his room in a home for the elderly, operated by the Little Sisters of the Poor in Cincinnati.

"They'd always want to know about themselves, about wealth, their love affairs, their health and everything. Some would ask me things I wouldn't tell them. They'd say, 'Is my husband true to me?'

"I wouldn't tell them that. Even if I saw it I wouldn't tell them. Another thing I wouldn't tell is if somebody stole something from them. I wouldn't tell them who stole it, but a lot of times I could might near tell who it was, if I wanted to."

Clippings dating to 1971 in The Courier-Journal archives tell of Morris being asked to help find missing children.

185

A Mrs. Homer McGuffin of Hardin Springs in Hardin County related how Morris directed searchers to her missing 2-year-old son, John, after he wandered away from the family farm in 1946.

Nearly 1,000 searchers, including 500 soldiers from Fort Knox, had failed to find the child when someone suggested that the mother consult Morris. He described exactly the path the child had taken, and told her that her son would be found under a cliff, near a pool of water.

A neighbor of the Mc-Guffins' heard Morris' description of the site and recognized it as a place on his farm.

Searchers found the child there, unharmed, and Mrs. McGuffin credited Morris with saving her son's life.

"A man stole a truck once and got away with it, and the law come to me and wanted me to tell them where it was," Morris said. "I told them that they had it hidden behind a barn, painting it, and where it was. And they went there, and there it was."

Countless such mysterious works have been attributed to Morris over the years, and, although he is still alert, most of what he has done has faded from his memory.

"I don't do things much that way now, like I used to," he said. "Nobody asks me things anymore. Age is against me."

For a few years in Munfordville, Morris had a license to charge a fee for his work, "and I got a right smart money then," he said. But for the most part his advice has been free, and those who came to him for advice gave him a little pocket change or a small gift in return for his services.

He now draws a small welfare check, which he gives to the Little Sisters of the Poor in return for the care he receives.

He was married once, years ago, but divorced, and he now has no living relatives, except a stepson and some stepgrandchildren who live far away.

"What hurts is when you get old and don't have anybody," he said. "I've had a miserable life. I always could help other people, but I never could help myself."

A couple of people in Cincinnati have befriended him, and often visit and read to him.

Otherwise, nuns at the Little Sisters of the Poor say that Morris spends most of his time praying and fasting, and smoking his pipe.

"The doctor told me that a pipe would do me more good than any medicine I could take," Morris said. "I'd rather have tobacco as to have money.

"I don't believe, with all that's wrong with me . . . I'll be here much more than a year, and I'd like to have enough tobacco to last me a year."

Bayou de Chien

June 2, 1993

HICKMAN, Ky. -- Bayou de Chien had already been named when early survey parties visited Western Kentucky in 1785.

Legend has it that the bayou's name, which means "creek of the dog," was given to the waterway by early French explorers on the Mississippi River, who were fascinated by the Indian dogs they saw in the vicinity.

The bayou -- which is pronounced "By-du-Shay" by local people -- originates in southwestern Graves County, just north of Pilot Oak. From there it meanders through the southern half of Hickman County and northern Fulton County, then meets the Mississippi at Hickman. Nearby, the remains of a 4 1/2-mile-long canal connect the bayou with Obion Creek. The canal appears to have been dug by hand, but there are no records of its construction in the county's history, and folklore has it that the canal is prehistoric.

Once upon a time, Bayou de Chien (which some maps spell Bayou du Chien) flowed uninterrupted all the way through the region that now is Reelfoot Lake and emptied into the Mississippi to the west of what is now Ridgely, Tenn., said Bill Threlkeld, a Fulton County historian who often lectures and shows slides about the bayou.

Threlkeld believes that in prehistoric times the Mississippi River channel at Hickman was farther west, in what is now Missouri. He is convinced that a few centuries ago -- well before the great New Madrid Earthquake of 1812 -- the river shifted closer to its present course and that since then the bayou has emptied into the Mississippi at Hickman.

188

He notes that while the Mississippi River makes a big loop below
Hickman, then actually runs north for a while around Madrid Bend,
the bayou's original path through Western Kentucky and west Tennessee enabled early river travelers in smaller boats to use the bayou
both as a shortcut to save time and to avoid interference from a
Spanish fort in the bend.

The cypress-shaded channel of the old south end of the bayou
still runs through the bottom lands near the Kentucky-Tennessee line,
and from the air, Threlkeld says, the remnants of the channel can be
seen snaking through Reelfoot Lake. The still-active portion of the
bayou between Hickman and Graves County could be described as a
fairly large creek in some areas. Its spring-fed channel has been
straightened on many farms, but in other places, cypress and willow
and an occasional beaver lodge help the bayou live up to its name.

The U.S. Fish and Wildlife Service says that the Bayou de Chien
watershed is the only place in the world where a tiny fish known as
the relict darter is known to live. The agency has proposed
endangered status for the rare fish that lives in the unusual stream.

"I don't guess it's too uncommon in the Mississippi Valley for
tributaries of the river to have French names, but I don't know of any
other one in Kentucky that has," said Lon Carter Barton, a respected
Graves County historian. "There's a small church in the southwest
corner of the county named Bayou de Chien Cumberland
Presbyterian Church. I think it was started in the 1830s."

Although Bayou de Chien is indisputably the best-known bayou in
Kentucky, William A. Withington, professor emeritus of geography
at the University of Kentucky and author of "Kentucky in Maps,"
says it is not the state's only bayou. Livingston County, on the Ohio
River just east of its confluence with the Mississippi, has both a
settlement and a creek named Bayou. And Bath County in
northeastern Kentucky has a Bayou Creek tributary of the Licking
River.

Dr. Hook

June 22, 1988

CALVERT CITY, Ky. -- A Western Kentucky physician has a most unusual method of collecting artificial lures -- by surgically removing them from fishermen.

Dr. Carroll W. Traylor, who has a family practice and does minor outpatient surgery at his clinic in Marshall County, says he has been saving artificial lures, fishhooks and a few other objects that he has extracted from his patients since about 1958.

He now has about 300 such items -- many taken from anglers who hooked themselves while fishing on nearby Kentucky Lake -- mounted for display in his examining room.

"They're really just for conversation," the doctor said. "I really don't fish very much at all.

"The majority of them have been removed from adults, but there are quite a few kids who are hooked by their cousins, their sisters or brothers or their parents, when they're in a boat and someone's coming back to cast and doesn't think about them."

In addition to artificial baits, Traylor's collection also contains dozens of plain fishhooks and treble hooks.

Then there's a 1 1/2-inch piece of wire that lodged in a young man's foot and went undetected for 12 years after he ran over it with a lawn mower.

And there are the zipper from a little boy's pants, a misguided frog gig that wound up in a human leg, a watercolor brush that was imbedded 4 1/4 inches deep in a little girl's face, and numerous other injurious relics that Traylor has removed.

He can recall, in detail, the story behind nearly every piece.

"Somewhere in there is a straight pin that this lady was holding in her mouth -- you've seen people do that when they were sewing -- and it went into her salivary gland. ...So I wouldn't recommend holding straight pins in your mouth," the doctor said.

Occasionally Traylor removes catfish spines from the feet of swimmers who have stepped on spines that have washed ashore after the catfish has perished. And sometimes he treats wounds suffered by fishermen who have been "horned" by the slightly venomous spines while handling live catfish.

"Commercial fishermen say the places don't become infected if you'll take some of that juice off the catfish and rub on the sting," Traylor said.

Usually he administers a local anesthetic before removing fishing lures from noses, ears and other body parts, but for patients who refuse anesthetic and choose to bite the bullet, Traylor keeps a battered Civil War bullet on a table in his examining room.

He suspects that tourist fishermen who have visited his clinic over the years have stolen a few of his better lures while his back was turned, but he is confident that -- what with his work at the clinic, plus frequent emergency-room duty at Marshall County Hospital and Lourdes Hospital in Paducah -- his collection will continue to grow.

"I make a deal with the patients," Traylor said. "I don't take the lure out unless they give it to me. It's as simple as that."

Chalk Dust Memories

February 13, 1989

BALD KNOB, KY. -- Goodness, it brought back memories the afternoon that I passed Bald Knob Elementary School in rural Franklin County and saw fresh chalk dust on the wall of the 50-year-old brick building.

It was as though someone had just pulled up beside me in a '57 Chevy -- with "Sixteen Candles" playing on the radio -- and handed me a double chocolate malt.

I heard the hiss of steam and the ominous clanking of pipes from the old iron radiators in the school I attended; smelled the scorched fragrance produced by steam heat, freshly oiled pine floors and, yes, chalk dust.

There is something Norman Rockwellian about children pounding erasers against the wall of a school.

Dusting erasers was one thing in school that I was good at. Washing blackboards was the other.

I felt pretty important when the teacher picked me -- and usually one other kid -- to dust erasers, always with a reminder: "Don't dust them on the building, only on the sidewalk."

"Yes, ma'am."

Some kids pounded erasers together to dust them, but the only way to do it right is to pound them against a hard surface. A sidewalk will do, but a brick wall is better.

Chalk and erasers fascinated me. There was something I liked about watching teachers use them -- the motion of their arms and hands, writing big words on the blackboard (our school had no green chalkboards), crossing t's and dotting i's, then making it all vanish with one long sweep of the eraser.

I could always tell when teachers were aggravated, because they wrote faster on the board, crossing t's and dotting i's more forcefully. Sometimes they wrote with such vengeance that it seemed their feet almost left the floor.

And when they broke the chalk, it usually meant that they, too, were nearly at the breaking point -- which brings me to my next subject, eraser fights.

It is a wonder that some of us didn't come down with white lung, as many eraser fights as we had. What fun they were! A fat, dusty eraser, flying through the air, bouncing off someone's head, chest or back. I can still hear the wonderful thump of a direct hit, with its explosion of chalk dust and the muffled giggles that ensued.

There was one unwritten rule for eraser fights at our school -- the teacher had to be out of the room.

She had just stepped out of algebra class one morning when someone hurled an eraser at another student.

It was the first throw of the grandest eraser fight that I ever witnessed. I am sure that I have blown the thing out of all reasonable proportions in my mind, but as I remember it, people threw erasers that morning who had never thrown them before and have never thrown them since.

Mild-mannered children who would not even make a paper airplane or whisper in class suddenly took up erasers against each other.

The fracas may have lasted only a few seconds, but it seemed an eternity of gleeful suspense, the kind that is distilled from disobedience and mischief in the face of stern authority.

It is a dreamlike memory to me now, possibly because it occurred nearly 30 years ago, but more likely because the fog of chalk dust in the classroom obscured visibility during the final moments of the fight.

Still, I recall with amazing clarity what happened to Bob Decker, who was seated two rows to my left, about halfway between the teacher's desk and the back wall.

I am sure that Bob had thrown his share of erasers that morning, but I do not remember what caused some members of the class to turn on him and, in their frenzy, pelt him about the head and shoulders with hand-held erasers until his hair, cut in a burr, turned solid white.

When the teacher returned seconds later, we all were working, straight-faced -- in a haze of chalk dust.

Because she was a strict disciplinarian, given only to levity of a mathematical nature, we feared the worst. But she took one look at Bob Decker's chalk-white head, turned away from the class and wrote some kind of equation on the board.

She wrote it slowly, deliberately and without much force -- like someone who was choking back laughter . . . or choking on chalk dust.

Falling into Fame

May 27, 1991

Chester Lamppin, 84, needed to set the record straight, he said. That's mostly why he was telling me this story.

It was in the fall of 1929, and a crowd of several thousand had gathered at Bowman Field in Louisville for an air show celebrating the opening of the Louisville Municipal Bridge (now called the Clark Memorial) over the Ohio River between Louisville and Jeffersonville, Ind.

Members of the Army Air Service 465th Pursuit Squadron, composed of local Army Reserve fliers in Louisville, were to do some stunts in the open-cockpit biplanes of that day. As the closing feature, a professional military parachutist was to jump from one of the planes.

Airplanes themselves were quite a novelty in the 1920s, and parachutes were an added attraction.

Naturally, when the parachutist didn't show up, the spectators were disappointed.

That's when Chester Lamppin, a 23-year-old staff sergeant -- an airplane mechanic who had never had any parachute training -- was told to make the jump.

"I'd been popping off about jumping and parachutes . . . and my commanding officer, Capt. F.E. Galloway, turned on me and said, 'All right, Lamppin, get your parachute on.'

"Before I could say anything . . . plump, they put this heavy jumper suit on me, and put the straps on. I looked over at my wife-to-be, and she said I turned white, green, blue and everything else. And before I knew it, I was up on the truck . . . and they drove it around all the people, and all the people were just applauding me and giving me the thunder," Lamppin recalled. "I wasn't prepared for it. I was kind of numb."

He was hoisted into the plane, which was piloted by the same commanding officer who had ordered him to jump.

"We never got along," Lamppin recalled. "He taxied the airplane around and let the crowd get a good look at me, then he gave it the gun and we went up."

There was a low ceiling that day, and Galloway leveled the plane off at 1,700 feet. It was not an ideal altitude for parachuting, but since Lamppin had never had one minute's instruction in jumping, he hardly had time to worry about its finer points.

Galloway throttled the engine and gave Lamppin the nod to jump.

"Now this was an open airplane, and you just climbed over the side and put your foot on a stirrup and the other one on the base of the wing where it meets the fuselage, and there was a gap in there where you could look down at the ground," Lamppin explained.

"I was standing there thinking, 'Well, I guess I might as well get this thing over with,' and all at once we flew over a graveyard, and all of those gravestones sticking straight up -- they had tall gravestones in those days -- and I looked down at it, and I said, 'That's an omen. I am not going to jump. I'm a coward. I'm going to climb back in. I just can't . . . . I'm going to get married in two months.' I was panting, you know." '

Lamppin scrambled to climb back into the plane, but couldn't.

"Things were jamming me all up. I couldn't get my leg up . . . and I was kind of excited anyway."

The ensuing seconds seemed an eternity as Lamppin pondered his desperate options.

"I got to thinking, 'If I just hung on the side here and they took me down on the river and flew right above the water (and let me jump), this suit might keep me up until they could come out and get me....' Then I said, 'No, I don't have a knife and can't cut loose.' "

All of a sudden, Lamppin was falling backward, watching the plane's tail-skid pass only inches from his head.

He pulled the ripcord and felt the wonderful jolt of the chute opening.

"I looked down at the ground and it was coming up pretty fast, and horns were blowing and people were screaming down there, and there were photographers, and I thought, 'My goodness.' " He landed near the airfield in several inches of mud, unhurt, and soon a truck came to pick him up.

"Lo and behold, they had my wife-to-be up in there . . . and they drove that truck around all that 10,000 people again. And that was my day in glory," Lamppin said.

Someone at the airfield gave him $50, which he used as a payment on an engagement ring for Muriel Wigginton, with whom he spent the next 59 years and raised a son and daughter.

Muriel died in December 1989, and Lamppin, a native of Floyds Knobs, Ind., still lives in Mobile, Ala., where he retired in 1963 as a civilian Air Force employee.

"Here's the whole thing," said Lamppin, during an interview on a visit to Louisville a few days ago. "Everybody thought I jumped, but I just fell off. And I've kept it a secret all these years. . . .

"I just thought maybe I'd better tell somebody."

Ice Sisters

August 2, 1991

BOSTON, Ky. -- Pink roses grow beside the rickety gate in front of the Ice sisters' aged two-story farmhouse.

Their mother planted the roses in the fall of 1918 when she had a going-away party for many of the boys in the community who were leaving for France to help fight World War I.

"The boys' girlfriends had roses that they wore on their dresses and left in the house after the dance, and my mother planted them out there, under jars. We've had them ever since," Catherine Ice said.

It is one of the many scenes that Catherine, 80, and her sister, Lucille, 79, have pressed in their scrapbook of memories from life on the farm that has been in the Ice family since soon after the Revolutionary War.

"We had a good time when we were kids," Catherine recalled. "Every night, before bedtime, our mother would read us a great big story out of the Tri-Weekly Constitution. I think it was a Georgia paper."

Neither Catherine, Lucille nor their older sister, Mary Elizabeth, 83, who still lives with them but is in ill health, ever married, because, as Catherine put it, "We were having too good a time to settle down."

Lucille remembered their school days, when she and Catherine were students at the one-room Ice Town School, some two miles away over the shortcut that they took, on foot, through the fields.

"They used to have us make soup for dinner in the wintertime, and one day the teacher had me to stir it, and I was holding a big chalkboard eraser in one hand and let it fall in the soup," Lucille said. "I took a pencil and got it out, and the teacher never did know it. But the soup was a little milky-looking."

The eraser incident is only one of many amusing tales that have followed the Ice sisters through life.

For a while, Lucille and Catherine milked 17 cows twice a day, by hand. One of the cows got her head caught between the rungs of a ladder that led to the barn loft, and the sisters set about trying to free the animal.

"Oh my goodness, she had her old horns hung in there, and we didn't have sense enough to saw the ladder in two. We tried to saw her horns off," Catherine said. "We had the awfullest time ever was."

After their parents died -- their mother, Alice, in 1943, and their father, Samuel, in 1952 -- the sisters and one of their three brothers continued to live on the 257-acre farm at the end of a long country lane.

One of their brothers was killed in a traffic accident while still young; another married and left the farm. Lucille looked after many of the chores and cooked for hired hands on the farm, and Catherine worked for many years at a sewing factory, then at a local distillery.

These days, the farmland is leased out and Lucille and Catherine take care of their older sister, tend to gardening and such, and sit on the shady front porch where they played as children.

At night, the big trees in their yard are full of roosting peacocks, between 85 and 100 of them, that have grown up in the woods along a stream behind their house.

It all started, they say, when two of the birds strayed onto their property from a neighboring farm, and never left.

Catherine gathered a few pictures of her brothers and sisters in their younger days, and Lucille told how she loved to dance back then.

"That was the old car that I learned to drive in," said Catherine, pointing to a Model A Ford in the background of one of the pictures.

It reminded Lucille of the time she and Catherine were taking a load of about 25 dozen eggs to market in the car when the brakes failed.

"We went up the road toward New Haven and there was a long hill with a creek at the bottom, full of rocks, and when Catherine came to that creek, she never had a bit of brake," Lucille said. "She went just ram, bang down in that creek, and I've never seen such a mess of busted up eggs in all my life.

"When we got over to the garage where the man could work on the brakes, eggs were dripping down through the bottom of the car right where he was working."

Catherine and Lucille were still laughing when they waved goodbye to me at the rickety yard gate where the pink roses grow.

The Pear Tree

December 4, 1991

It was never very pretty, even for a pear tree, and it was completely out of place. Pear trees have a way of growing where they shouldn't, you know.

I never hear that line about "a partridge in a pear tree" in the Christmas song that I don't picture this tree in my mind.

From the earliest I can remember, the tree stood practically in the middle of the field on a farm that belonged to my uncle George, next to our place.

No one ever knew how it came to be there, in a low spot, near the skeleton of an old

fence row. The tree was always kind of a loner. Its only companion all these years has been a weather-beaten fence post that stands a few feet away.

I never recall trying to climb the tree. It did not ask to be climbed. But often I stopped at the tree when I was a kid, and thought it odd that a pear tree should be sitting by itself in the middle of nowhere.

Never was it mentioned around our place, except as a point of reference for directions, as in "over by the pear tree," or "just past the pear tree." It produced pears every summer, but none fit to eat.

I loved pears, and always nurtured the hope that one day I would find a big yellow, soft, juicy pear dangling from one of the limbs on the old pear tree, but that was a fantasy.

Its pears were rock-hard and the color of rust, and there was some talk that they might contain metal.

Yet I never failed to visit the tree a few times each year, hoping for a miracle; believing that one day, if only by accident, an edible piece of fruit might grow from the scrubby limbs.

201

I always suspected that the tree and the aged fence post nearby were somehow connected underground. All the other fence posts that once must have stood in a row were gone, even when I was a boy. Only that one post near the pear tree never seemed to grow older.

I left them there, the pear tree and the old fence post, when I went away to school many years ago, then took a job in the city.

About the only times I ever thought of the tree were when I got hold of a bad pear from the store, or when I heard the Christmas song.

I'd have guessed time and the elements should long since have disposed of the post and the pear tree. But when I looked in on them a few days ago, there they were -- the agrarian odd couple -- looking pretty much as they had when I left them.

I got out my camera and snapped a picture of the two.

Then I circled the tree and looked it over closely, marveling at its longevity. There in the top branches hung two or three little petrified pears that must have been from this year's crop.

Then again, they may have been the same ones that were hanging up there when I left, years ago.

A Few Strands of Lights

November 8, 1991

The fifth of November may have been a bit early for Christmas lights, but there they were -- several strings of them -- burning brightly on the tiny porch of a modest hillside home.

The night was moonless, cold and blustery. It was late, and a friend and I were on our way back from an interview in Southern Kentucky, listening to stale wrap-ups of election returns on the radio. Christmas lights were a welcome sight and a pleasant diversion from politics.

Maybe it was not too early for Christmas lights after all, we agreed.

There had been snowflakes from low, gray clouds for two or three days now, and we figured there were children in the house; little ones, who took the snowflakes and cold wind to mean that Christmas must be just around the corner.

We decided there was a young mother inside with the children gathered around her, listening to Christmas songs and looking at toys they'd picked out in a tattered mail-order catalog.

Would she laugh apologetically about turning the lights on this early, then explain that the children were so excited about Christmas that she could not resist hanging the strands and playing the Christmas music, just to see the sparkle in their eyes?

Might she scold her husband for his good-natured grumbling about the lights? And would she whisper that there wasn't going to be much money for Christmas this year, and that she didn't think it would hurt to let the kids start enjoying the season a little early?

I guess we should not have seen so much through the glow around the little house, but we could not help believing -- perhaps because we needed to -- that inside there lived a most fortunate family:

Children whose parents gave them the gift of imagination -- of dreaming of Christmas when the first snowflakes tumbled from the sky; of finding a toy shop in the pages of a worn-out mail-order catalog; of wishing upon the stars they saw in the Christmas lights that their mother strung across the porch the first week in November.

We wished we had been there when the lights were plugged in, to see the children's noses pressed against the windows and to hear their hearts pounding.

They would get something this Christmas, we agreed, that cannot be bought in stores -- sweet memories of childhood and a cozy feeling inside that children have when they are truly loved.

No grand display that I will see this holiday season will so warm my spirit as those few strings of lights that shone from the porch of the little house on a lonesome hillside, on the cold night of Nov. 5.

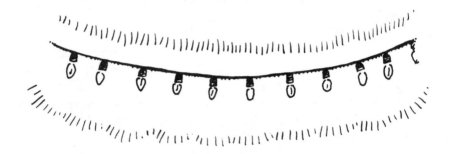

How Santa Scored a Touchdown

December 24, 1984

Once upon a Christmas list, a little boy wrote that he wanted only one toy: a Dallas Cowboys football helmet.

Santa winced as he read the letter, for he had never seen a Dallas helmet, except on a Dallas Cowboy. And not even jolly old Saint Nick was game enough to ask one of those guys for his helmet.

Christmas was fast approaching, and Santa grew uneasy. He wanted more than anything to find a helmet, for he loved the little boy like a son.

Finally, a few days before Christmas, one of Santa's helpers told of seeing helmets of several professional football teams in the Sears catalog, and Santa's hopes brightened.

Maybe there was a chance.

The local Sears Roebuck and Co. store did not handle the helmets, but maybe if Santa called the Chicago office, the catalog sales department could find one.

No, they had all been sold, he was told, and there was virtually no chance of finding one before Christmas.

Not since the heavy fog, when Rudolph came to the rescue, had Santa faced such a dilemma. Yet he would not give up.

He called the Dallas Cowboys' general offices in Texas and poured out his plight to a sympathetic secretary who checked around the office, then suggested that he phone a place in Dallas called "Toy World."

A few minutes later, Santa poured out his story to a kind lady -- with grandchildren -- who worked in the helmet department at the toy store.

Yes, she had a few Cowboys helmets left, she said, and she was touched by Santa's story.

Did he have a charge card?

Of course he had a charge card. Who could shop for Christmas without one?

He gave her the card number, and she crossed her heart and swore on a picture of Tom Landry that she would put the helmet on the next sleigh out of Dallas.

Just in time for Christmas, the helmet -- which now had cost almost as much in phone calls and shipping as an entire uniform -- arrived at Santa's humble but happy headquarters.

Santa unwrapped it, looked it over and paused for a moment to thank God for telephones, charge cards, secretaries and sales clerks who have grandchildren.

The sparkle in the little boy's eyes shone as brightly as the lights on the tree when he stumbled -- half asleep, his heart racing -- through the darkness of Christmas morning to see what Santa had left.

The Dallas Cowboys helmet was there, just as he had known it would be.

In the days and months that followed, it bobbed across the yard on many imaginary touchdown runs. Sometimes it was worn by a tackle or a linebacker; sometimes by a quarterback, waiting coolly in the face of a blitz to release a game-winning bomb.

The seasons flew by and a few short years later Santa found the helmet lying in a forgotten corner of the yard, fading in the weather on the once make-believe football field.

The tousled head it once protected now was cluttered with thoughts of girls, college and a career.

How quickly the boy had grown. No longer did he write letters to Santa, or scramble breathlessly from his bed at 5:30 on Christmas morning. His imagination, like the star on the aging Cowboys helmet, had faded.

Wonderful, perhaps. But somehow sad to old Santa.

What a shame for Santa that childhood must end. For he misses the little boy's letters.

A Legacy of Giving

December 25, 1991

LOUISVILLE, Ky. -- What the world really needs for Christmas is a few more people like William and Anna Lee Blincoe.

Some of the Blincoes' nine children remember protesting, as youngsters, when their parents made them share Christmas gifts with less fortunate children in the neighborhood near the housing project where they lived.

As they grew older, however, the children found the same joy in helping others that William and Anna Lee Blincoe had discovered years earlier. So began the Blincoe family legacy of giving; a legacy warmer than the coziest Christmas hearth, and brighter than the prettiest tree.

"Hard times taught me a lesson," 78-year-old Anna Lee Blincoe said. "What started us off trying to do something to help somebody else was because people were really nice to us back in the 1930s when we were hit real hard. We decided that so many people had been so nice to us when our children were small . . . that if we ever got able, we would share with other people who were just in the same boat we were in."

Since the 1950s, William and Anna Lee Blincoe have been fixing up old toys, mending clothes and saving money with their children and friends to help poor people of all races who are in need at Christmas and throughout the year.

"One year . . . me and my husband and my brother, Ed Rodgers, went to a house where these people's gas and lights were off. But their house was as clean as a pin," Anna Lee Blincoe recalled. "There were about seven children -- two little twins -- and all the gifts they had were just what some of the children had gotten from school. They didn't have a tree, just a few little things on top of a radiator.

"We didn't have enough toys for them, but while I was at midnight Mass, my brother, who had 11 children, went to his house and carried back toys and gifts from his tree to that family."

William and Anna Lee Blincoe seldom took much credit for the good they did, preferring instead to give God the credit.

William Blincoe, a delivery truck driver for a Louisville equipment company, was not in good health, and Anna Lee, who worked as a cook and housekeeper, had rheumatic fever as a child in Meade County and has been crippled with arthritis since age 12. She was bedfast for a time in the 1940s, and she has been confined to a wheelchair since 1985.

Two weeks before Christmas in 1989, William Blincoe died of a massive heart attack at age 76. He had been working for months, gathering up items for Christmas giving, and he had been especially concerned about getting them delivered early that year.

With William gone, Anna Lee feared that she wouldn't be able to continue collecting and distributing toys and clothing. But St. Raphael School on Bardstown Road called that Christmas, wanting names for its Angel tree, and Anna Lee gave them 54.

"Our Lord takes care of us," she explained. "Even though I can't walk, I can still use my hands. The blessings have outweighed the hardships. I am a millionaire and I don't have a penny in the bank."

Other than a small Social Security check, Anna Lee Blincoe's income comes from working at her sewing machine, making clothing, dolls, Christmas ornaments, placemats, potholders and other items.

But from her wheelchair, she holds together a growing network of giving that reaches far beyond her modest two-story home on River Park Drive in Louisville's West End. Two of her daughters, Frances Spinks, a social worker, and Mary Brown, a teacher, say they have often sent to their mother "people who have fallen through the cracks" and have nowhere to turn for help.

"I'd like for people to pick up the idea and carry it into other neighborhoods, so nobody would be forgotten," Anna Lee Blincoe said.

"My children go out and find people and take them clothes and food, and sometimes they'll come here and say, 'Mother, I need such-and-such a thing, because there's an old man up here with no clothes. . . .'

"My husband took off one of his best coats one time -- because he wasn't going out too much -- and gave it to one of the people that my son had found."

The Blincoe family really knows how to celebrate Christmas.

The Chair that Came Back

January 6, 1993

Clay and Velma Lykins were turning out their Christmas lights on the night of Dec. 20 when they noticed a large object covered with plastic at the end of their driveway in southern Jefferson County.

Clay was astonished to find a wicker rocking chair that had been stolen from their porch about 18 years earlier.

Taped to the cushion -- the same hunter green one that was on the chair when it was stolen -- was an unsigned, typewritten note:

"To whom this may concern: Approximately 15 to 17 years ago my husband stole this wicker rocking chair from the porch of this house. I am ashamed of this behavior and am returning this stolen item. I have been divorced from my husband for twelve years and have since been 'born-again.' My life has completely changed and I want to undo any wrongdoing to the best of my ability. I know this chair is not in the same condition as when it was stolen, and I apologize. I now live in another state, Tennessee, and am rarely if ever in this vicinity. I realize the cowardly fashion in which I am returning this, but the reason is obvious. I will not bother you again. Please forgive us. Sincerely,"

Clay and Velma Lykins sat at their kitchen table, reading the letter in amazement. "We just looked at each other," Clay said. "I got goose bumps at first, and almost got tears in my eyes when I realized what a change had taken place. It's touching."

Remembering that his insurance company had made at least partial restitution for the stolen chairs -- the wicker rocker and a straight-backed wicker chair, which was not returned and was not mentioned in the note -- Clay phoned the insurance claims office the

210

next day to explain that one of the chairs had been returned and that he wanted to repay part of the claim.

"I still haven't heard from the insurance company. Someone told me that they probably don't want to fool with this, because they don't have any procedure for doing it," he said.

Neither Clay, a retired Jefferson County school principal, nor Velma, a retired teacher, has any idea who might have stolen the chair.

"We thought, at the time, that it was probably just some youngsters," Velma said.

"This person said the chair was stolen 'from the porch of this house,' " Clay said, "so we don't know if this person even knew that we still lived here."

The Lykinses don't plan to return the long-lost wicker rocker to the porch. Instead, it will be placed in a guest bedroom, they say, and with it, the simple, sincere letter of apology that made Christmas 1992 especially memorable for them.

"It's the thing that will stand out in my mind as long as I live," Clay said.

"I would love to have met this lady," Velma said. "That would have made it complete."

A Little Girl's Gift

December 25, 1987

This story took place one week ago today, in an elementary school in rural Central Kentucky. The teacher agreed to share the story but asked that the school, teacher and student not be identified out of respect for the privacy of the family.

The third-grade classroom was abuzz with excitement as the teacher opened her gifts, pausing to admire the beautiful wrapping paper and ribbons, thanking each student by name.

Suddenly someone mentioned that an 8-year-old classmate was in the cloakroom crying.

The teacher thought she had seen the little girl put a gift under the Christmas tree, but it was not there when the gifts were opened.

While the other children celebrated, the teacher approached the blonde-haired, blue-eyed girl to see what was wrong.

"Didn't you have a gift for me?" the teacher whispered.

Tearfully, the child nodded that she did.

"Don't you want to give it to me?"

The child shook her head, then said, sobbing, "Mine's not pretty."

"Well, now, why don't you let me be the judge of that," the teacher consoled her.

With tears streaming down her face, the child handed the teacher her present. It was wrapped in pink wallpaper with little flowers, and no ribbon.

The teacher began to cry as she looked at the wallpaper, and at the tears in the eyes of the little girl who had worked so hard to make her gift a pretty one, but who had been ashamed to leave it under the tree with the others.

The teacher remembered that, a few days earlier, when all the students brought gifts to take to a local nursing home, the child's gift had been a little bar of motel soap, wrapped in notebook paper and fastened with adhesive tape, with the words, "To a friend, love ...," written on the outside.

She also had realized that the child, who came from a poor family, was very special during the nursing home visit. The youngster

212

had noticed an old woman crying in a room by herself and had left the other children to go in and visit.

"It doesn't matter what's in a package, " the teacher told the child. "All I ask of you for Christmas is your love, and you've already given me that. So if you didn't give me anything else, that would be enough.

"That was when she grabbed me around the neck, and just hugged my neck and cried and cried. We both shed quite a few tears there."

When the teacher opened the gift, inside the pink wallpaper, she found a Lipton teabag box and, inside it, wrapped in a small blue hand towel, two little glass votive cups -- with dust gathered around their candles -- that the little girl had found at home and thought the teacher would like.

"Mama wrapped them up in the towel to keep them from breaking," she said.

The teacher choked back tears as she thanked the child for the wonderful gift, and promised her that she had a perfect place for it at her house.

It was, she reflected, perhaps the most touching moment of her 27 years in the classroom.

A little girl who had no money to buy a gift, and no wrapping paper or ribbon, had reminded her once again that a gift of love is far too valuable for a price tag, and that the most beautiful presents of all are often wrapped in the plainest paper.

The teacher found a perfect place for the child's candles, right beside the little nativity scene on a table in her home.

Merry Christmas to you all.